My Google®
Nexus™ 7 and Nexus™ 10

Craig James Johnston

que®

800 East 96th Street,
Indianapolis, Indiana 46240 USA

My Google Nexus™ 7 and Nexus™ 10

Copyright © 2013 by Pearson Education, Inc.

ISBN-13: 978-0-7897-5045-7

ISBN-10: 0-7897-5045-7

Library of Congress Cataloging-in-Publication data is on file.

First Printing: January 2013

Trademarks

All terms mentioned in this book that are known to be trademarks or service marks have been appropriately capitalized. Que Publishing cannot attest to the accuracy of this information. Use of a term in this book should not be regarded as affecting the validity of any trademark or service mark.

Warning and Disclaimer

Every effort has been made to make this book as complete and as accurate as possible, but no warranty or fitness is implied. The information provided is on an "as is" basis. The author and the publisher shall have neither liability nor responsibility to any person or entity with respect to any loss or damages arising from the information contained in this book.

Bulk Sales

Que Publishing offers excellent discounts on this book when ordered in quantity for bulk purchases or special sales. For more information, please contact

U.S. Corporate and Government Sales

1-800-382-3419

corpsales@pearsontechgroup.com

For sales outside of the U.S., please contact

International Sales

international@pearsoned.com

Editor-in-Chief
Greg Wiegand

Acquisitions Editor
Michelle Newcomb

Development Editor
Charlotte Kughen, The Wordsmithery LLC

Managing Editor
Sandra Schroeder

Project Editor
Seth Kerney

Indexer
Ken Johnson

Proofreader
Kathy Ruiz

Technical Editor
Vince Averello

Editorial Assistant
Cindy Teeters

Book Designer
Anne Jones

Compositor
MPS Limited

Contents at a Glance

Table of Contents

About the Author

Craig James Johnston has been involved with technology since his high school days at Glenwood High in Durban, South Africa, when his school was given some Apple][Europluses. From that moment technology captivated him, and he has owned, supported, evangelized, and written about it.

Craig has been involved in designing and supporting large-scale enterprise networks with integrated email and directory services since 1989. He has held many different IT-related positions in his career ranging from sales support engineer to mobile architect for a 40,000-smartphone infrastructure at a large bank.

In addition to designing and supporting mobile computing environments, Craig co-hosts the CrackBerry.com podcast, as well as guest hosting on other podcasts including iPhone and iPad Live podcasts. You can see Craig's previously published work in his books *Professional BlackBerry*, and many books in the *My* series, including *My BlackBerry Curve*, *My Palm Pre*, *My Nexus One*, *My DROID* (first and second editions), *My Motorola Atrix 4G*, *My BlackBerry PlayBook*, *My HTC EVO 3D*, and *My Samsung Galaxy Nexus*.

Craig also enjoys high-horsepower, high-speed vehicles and tries very hard to keep to the speed limit while driving them.

Originally from Durban, South Africa, Craig has lived in the United Kingdom, the San Francisco Bay Area, and New Jersey, where he now lives with his wife, Karen, and a couple of cats.

Craig would love to hear from you. Feel free to contact Craig about your experiences with *My Google Nexus 7 and Nexus 10* at http://www.CraigsBooks.info.

All comments, suggestions, and feedback are welcome, including positive and negative.

Dedication

I have noticed even people who claim everything is predestined, and that we can do nothing to change it, look before they cross the road.

—*Stephen Hawking*

Acknowledgments

I would like to express my deepest gratitude to the following people on the *My Google Nexus 7 and Nexus 10* team who all worked extremely hard on this book, including:

My agent, Carole Jelen; Michelle Newcomb, my acquisitions editor who worked with me to give this project an edge; and technical editor Vince Averello, development editor Charlotte Kughen, project editor Seth Kerney, indexer Ken Johnson, and proofreader Kathy Ruiz.

We Want to Hear from You!

As the reader of this book, *you* are our most important critic and commentator. We value your opinion and want to know what we're doing right, what we could do better, what areas you'd like to see us publish in, and any other words of wisdom you're willing to pass our way.

We welcome your comments. You can email or write to let us know what you did or didn't like about this book—as well as what we can do to make our books better.

Please note that we cannot help you with technical problems related to the topic of this book.

When you write, please be sure to include this book's title and author as well as your name and email address. We will carefully review your comments and share them with the author and editors who worked on the book.

Email: feedback@quepublishing.com

Mail: Que Publishing
             ATTN: Reader Feedback
             800 East 96th Street
             Indianapolis, IN 46240 USA

Reader Services

Visit our website and register this book at quepublishing.com/register for convenient access to any updates, downloads, or errata that might be available for this book.

Prologue

In this chapter, you become familiar with the external features of the Google Nexus Tablet and the basics of getting started with the Android operating system. Topics include the following:

→ Your Google Nexus Tablet's external features
→ Fundamentals of Android 4.1 (Jelly Bean)
→ First-time setup
→ Synchronization software

Getting to Know Your Google Nexus Tablet

Let's start by getting to know more about your Google Nexus Tablet by examining the external features, device features, and how Google's latest operating system, Android 4.2 (or Jelly Bean), works.

One important thing to remember about any Android tablet bearing the Nexus name is that it is a pure Android tablet with no wireless carrier or vendor modifications. Google, the company that makes Android, commissions Nexus tablets to have the latest features and run the latest version of Google's Android operating system, in this case Android 4.2, and Google insists that is the device uses the pure, unchanged version of Android.

Your Google Nexus Tablet's External Features

Becoming familiar with the external features of your Google Nexus Tablet is a good place to start because you will be using them often. This chapter also covers some of the technical specifications of your Google Nexus Tablet, including the touch screen and camera. There are two Google Nexus tablets: the Nexus 7 and the Nexus 10.

Nexus 7

Front

Light sensor   Adjusts the brightness of the screen based on the brightness of the ambient light.

Front camera   1.2 megapixel front-facing camera that you can use for video chat, taking self-portraits, and even unlocking your Google Nexus Tablet using your face.

Touchscreen   The Google Nexus Tablet has a 7"800 × 1280 pixel back-lit IPS (In-plane Switching) screen that incorporates 10-finger capacitive touch.

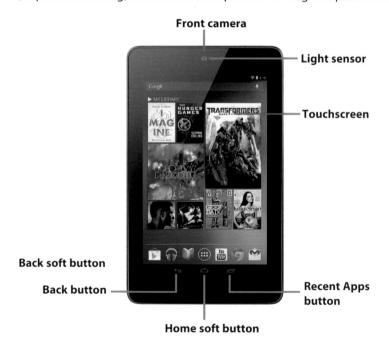

Front camera

Light sensor

Touchscreen

Back soft button

Back button

Recent Apps button

Home soft button

Back button   Touch to go back one screen when using an application or menu. This virtual button is actually on the screen.

Recent Apps button   Touch to see a list of recently used apps and switch between them. This virtual button is actually on the screen.

Home button   Touch to go to the Home screen. The application that you are using continues to run in the background. This virtual button is actually on the screen.

Back

Speaker   Produces audio for all apps, system sounds, and video and audio calls (using apps such as Skype and Google Talk).

Microphone   Used for video and audio calls (using apps such as Skype or Google Talk).

3.5 mm headphone jack   Used with third-party headsets so you can enjoy music and talk on the tablet.

Micro-USB port   Used to synchronize your Google Nexus Tablet to your desktop computer and charge it.

Microphone

Speaker

3.5 mm headphone jack

Micro-USB port

Left Side

Docking pins   Use with accessories and docks to automatically start certain applications and charge your Google Nexus Tablet. For example, a vehicle dock could automatically launch the Navigation app.

Right Side

Power button   Press once to wake your Google Nexus Tablet. Press and hold for one second to reveal a menu of choices. The choices enable you to put your Google Nexus Tablet into silent mode, airplane mode, or power it off completely.

Volume up/down buttons Control the audio volume on calls and while playing audio and video.

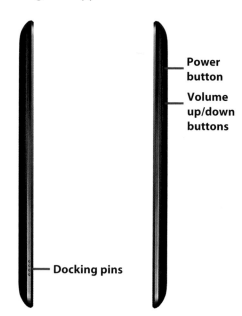

Power button

Volume up/down buttons

Docking pins

Nexus 10

Front

Power button   Press once to wake your Google Nexus Tablet. Press and hold for one second to reveal a menu of choices. The choices enable you to put your Google Nexus Tablet into silent mode, airplane mode, or power it off completely.

Volume up/down buttons   Control the audio volume on calls and while playing audio and video.

Light sensor   Adjusts the brightness of the screen based on the brightness of the ambient light.

Front camera   1.9-megapixel front-facing camera that you can use for video chat, taking self-portraits, and even unlocking your Google Nexus Tablet using your face.

Touchscreen   The Google Nexus Tablet has a 10.055" 1600 × 2560 pixel back-lit PLS LCD (Plane to Line Switching) screen that incorporates 10-finger capacitive touch.

Power **Volume up/** **Light** **Front**
button **down buttons** **sensor** **camera** **Touchscreen**

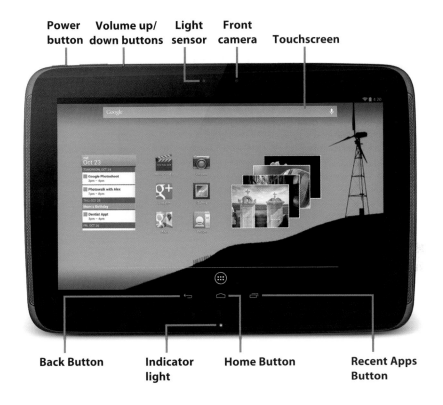

Back Button   **Indicator**   **Home Button**   **Recent Apps**
                       light   **Button**

Back button   Touch to go back one screen when using an application or menu. This virtual button is actually on the screen.

Recent Apps button   Touch to see a list of recently used apps and switch between them. This virtual button is actually on the screen.

Home button   Touch to go to the Home screen. The application that you are using continues to run in the background. This virtual button is actually on the screen.

Indicator light   Indicates new events (such as new email). The light can be any color combination of red, green, or blue (RGB) so different apps can use different colors of alerts.

Speakers   Stereo speakers that are used when you play music, movies, or talk on Skype and other video chat apps.

Back

Rear camera   5-megapixel camera with autofocus takes clear pictures close-up or far away.

LED (Light Emitting Diode) camera flash   Helps to illuminate the surroundings when taking pictures in low light.

Microphone   This microphone is used when you record videos.

3.5 mm headphone jack   Used with third-party headsets so you can enjoy music and talk on the tablet.

Micro-USB port   Used to synchronize your Google Nexus Tablet to your desktop computer and charge it.

Micro-HDMI port   Used with an HDMI or Micro-HDMI cable to connect your tablet to a TV to watch movies or mirror what is on the screen.

Bottom

Docking pins   Used with accessories, docks to automatically start certain applications, and to charge your Google Nexus Tablet. For example, a vehicle dock could automatically launch the Navigation app.

Other Sensors and Radios

Your Google Nexus tablet includes a Wi-Fi (WLAN) radio that supports 802.11 b/g/n for connecting to your home or office networks or to Wi-Fi hotspots in airports, coffee shops, and even on planes. It also has a Bluetooth V3.0 radio for connecting Bluetooth accessories such as headsets, and a Near Field Communications (NFC) radio for mobile payments and swapping information between other Android devices. On the sensor front it has an accelerometer for detecting movement, a compass for directional awareness, gyroscope for assisting with movement detection and gaming, Global Positioning System (GPS) for detecting where you are on the planet, and a Hall Sensor for detecting a magnetic field.

First-Time Setup

Before setting up your new Samsung Google Nexus Tablet it is advisable you have a Google account. This is because your Google Nexus Tablet running Android is tightly integrated into Google and enables you to store your content in the Google cloud, including any books and music you buy or movies you rent. If you do not already have a Google account, head to https://accounts.google.com on your desktop computer and sign up for one.

You Need Wi-Fi to Set Up Your Nexus Tablet

You need to be able to connect to a Wi-Fi network when you set up your Google Nexus Tablet.

1. Touch and hold the Power button until you see the animation start playing.

2. Touch to change your location if needed.

3. Touch to start the setup process.

4. Select a Wi-Fi network to connect to.

5. Type in the Wi-Fi network password.

6. Touch Connect.

7. Touch Yes if you already have a Google account. Otherwise, touch No to create a Google account.

8. Enter your Google account username (which is your Gmail email address).

9. Enter your Google account password.

10. Touch to Sign In.

Touch to get a Google account

11. Check this box if you are switching from a previous Android tablet or smartphone and want to move all of your apps and settings to your new Google Nexus Tablet.

12. Check this box if you want your apps and settings to be backed up to the Google cloud.

13. Touch to go to the next screen.

14. Check this box if you are okay with Google collecting information about your geographic location at any time. Although Google keeps this information safe, if you are concerned about privacy rights you should uncheck this box.

15. Check this box if you are okay with Google using your geographic location for Google searches and other Google services such as navigation.

16. Touch to go to the next screen.

17. Touch to start using your Google Nexus tablet

Setting Up Multiple Users on Your Tablet

With the introduction of Android 4.2, Google has added the capability for your Android tablet to support multiple users. This allows you to share your tablet among co-workers, family members, or friends, and each of them will have their own unique login, apps, photos, videos, and settings. Your Android 4.2 or later-powered tablet can support up to eight users. To add a new user to your tablet, the new user must be present. The original owner of the tablet must be logged in and needs to follow these steps.

1. Touch the Settings icon.

2. Touch Users.

3. Touch Add User.

4. Touch OK.

5. Touch Set Up Now.

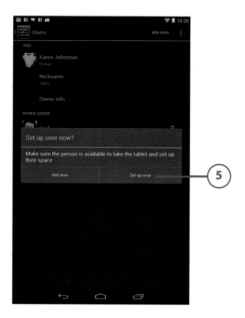

6. Hand the tablet to the person who will be setting up a new account.

7. Swipe the lock icon to start the new user setup process. Follow the steps in the previous section "First-Time Setup" to complete the setup of the new account.

New user icon
selected

Fundamentals of Android 4.2

Your Google Nexus Tablet is run by an operating system called Android. Android was created by Google to run on any tablet or smartphone, and there are quite a few tablets and smartphones that run on Android today. Your Google Nexus Tablet uses the latest version of Android, called Android 4.2 (or Jelly Bean). Let's go over how to use Android 4.1.

The Lock Screen

If you haven't used your Google Nexus Tablet for a while, the screen goes blank to conserve battery power. Here is how to interact with the Lock screen.

1. Press the Power button to wake up your Google Nexus Tablet.

2. Touch a user to choose who you want to log in as.

3. Slide the padlock icon in any direction, then release it to unlock your tablet.

Work with Notifications on the Lock Screen

With Android 4.2 you can work with notifications right on the lock screen. If you see notifications in the Notification bar, pull down the Notification bar to view and clear them. Touching a notification takes you straight to the app that created them. Read more about the Notification bar later in this section.

Change settings right on the Lock Screen

With Android 4.2, you can now pull down a Quick Notifications menu that allows you to change things such as screen brightness, which Wi-Fi network you want to connect to, the Auto-rotate setting, and Battery settings.

Open Google Now

With Android 4.2, you can swipe up from the bottom of the screen to open Google Now. We will cover more about Google Now in Chapter 6, "Google Now and Navigation."

The Home Screen(s)

After you unlock your Google Nexus Tablet, you are presented with the middle Home screen. Your Google Nexus Tablet has five Home screens. The Home screens contain application shortcuts, a Launcher icon, Notification Bar, Shortcuts, Favorites Tray, and widgets.

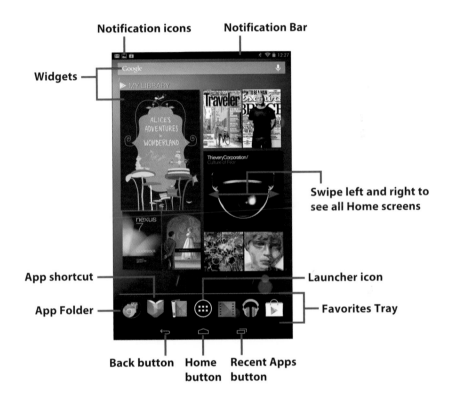

Notification icons   **Notification Bar**

Widgets

Swipe left and right to see all Home screens

App shortcut   **Launcher icon**

App Folder   **Favorites Tray**

**Back button   Home   Recent Apps
button   button**

Notification Bar   The Notification Bar shows information about Bluetooth, Wi-Fi, and cellular coverage, as well as the battery level and time. The Notification Bar also serves as a place where apps can alert or notify you using notification icons.

Notification icons   Notification icons appear in the Notification Bar when an app needs to alert or notify you of something. For example, the Tablet app can show the missed call icon indicating that you missed a call.

App Folders   App Folders are groups of apps that you can use to organize apps and declutter your screen.

Widgets Widgets are applications that run right on the Home screens. They are specially designed to provide functionality and real-time information. An example of a widget is one that shows the current weather or provides search capability. You can move and resize widgets.

App shortcut Touching an app shortcut launches the associated app.

Working with Notifications

To interact with notifications that appear in the Notification Bar, place your finger above the top-left of the screen and drag it down to reveal the notifications. Swipe each individual notification off the screen to the left or right to clear them one by one. Using two fingers, drag down on a notification to expand it.

Touch to launch the associated app   **Touch to clear all notifications**

Working with Quick Settings

In Android 4.2 and later, Google has introduced a new pull-down bar called Quick Settings. To interact with the Quick Settings bar, place your finger above the top-right of the screen and drag it down to reveal it.

Touch to
switch users

Rotation Lock
on/off

Touch to open the
full Settings screen

Pull down the
Notification Bar

Creating App Shortcuts

Touch the Launcher icon to see all of your apps. Touch and hold on the app you want to make a shortcut for. After the Home screens appear, drag the app shortcut to where you want it on the Home screen, drag it to an App folder to add it to the folder, or drag it left or right off the screen to move it between Home screens. Release the icon to place it.

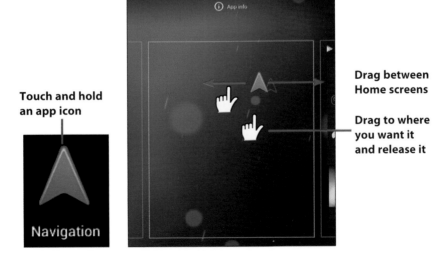

Touch and hold
an app icon

Drag between
Home screens

Drag to where
you want it
and release it

Creating App Folders

To create a new App Folder, simply drag one app shortcut onto another one. An App Folder is created automatically. To name your new App Folder, touch the folder to open it and touch Unnamed Folder to enter your own name.

**Drag one icon onto another
to make a folder**

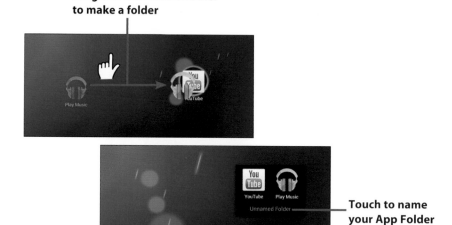

**Touch to name
your App Folder**

Favorites Tray   The Favorites Tray is visible on all five Home screens. You can drag apps to the Favorites Tray so that they are available no matter which Home screen you are looking at. You can rearrange and move apps in the Favorites Tray.

Launcher icon   Touch to show application icons for all applications that you have installed on your Google Nexus Tablet.

The System Bar

Your Google Nexus Tablet running Android 4.1 has no physical buttons. Instead it has an area of the screen set aside for virtual buttons. This area is called the System Bar. The System Bar includes the Back, Home, and Recent Apps virtual buttons.

Home button   **Recent Apps button**

Back button

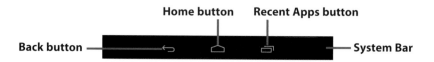

System Bar

System Bar   Reserved area of the screen where virtual buttons are displayed.

Back button   Touch to go back one screen in an app or back one step while navigating Android.

Home button   Touch to exit what you are doing and return to the Home screen. Your app continues to run in the background.

Recent Apps button   Touch to see your recently used apps, switch between them, and close them.

Vanishing System Bar

Some apps can dim or hide the System Bar to provide a little extra screen real estate. When this happens, the virtual buttons are still there, however, they are reduced to very dim dots.

Home button

Back button ⎯⎯⎯⎯⎯  ⎯⎯⎯⎯⎯ **Recent Apps button**

Where Is the Menu Button?

If you are familiar with previous versions of Android, you know there used to be a Menu button. This Menu button provided contextual actions for the app you were using. In Android 4.0 (Ice Cream Sandwich) and Android 4.1 (Jelly Bean), the Menu button has been moved to the upper-right of the screen when it is needed within an app. The Menu button is now three vertical dots. Sometimes this virtual Menu button might appear in the System Bar to the right of the Recent Apps button.

Menu Button

Using Your Touchscreen

Interacting with your Google Nexus Tablet is done mostly by touching the screen—what's known as making gestures on the screen. You can touch, swipe, pinch, double-tap, and type.

Touch   To start an application, touch its icon. Touch a menu item to select it. Touch the letters of the onscreen keyboard to type.

Touch and hold   Touch and hold to interact with an object. For example, if you touch and hold a blank area of the Home screen, a menu pops up. If you touch and hold an icon, you can reposition it with your finger.

Drag   Dragging always starts with a touch and hold. For example, if you touch the Notification Bar, you can drag it down to read all of the notification messages.

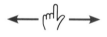

Swipe or slide   Swipe or slide the screen to scroll quickly. To swipe or slide, move your finger across the screen quickly. Be careful not to touch and hold before you swipe or you will reposition something. You can also swipe to clear notifications or close apps when viewing the recent apps.

Double-tap   Double-tapping is like double-clicking a mouse on a desktop computer. Tap the screen twice in quick succession. For example, you can double-tap a web page to zoom in to part of that page.

Pinch   To zoom in and out of images and pages, place your thumb and forefinger on the screen. Pinch them together to zoom out or spread them apart (unpinch) to zoom in. Applications such as Browser, Gallery, and Maps support pinching.

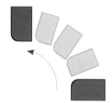

Rotate the screen   If you rotate your Google Nexus Tablet from an upright position to being on its left or right side, the screen switches from portrait view to landscape view. Most applications honor the screen orientation. The Home screens and Launcher do not.

Using Your Keyboard

Your Google Nexus Tablet has a virtual (onscreen) keyboard for those times when you need to enter text. You might be a little wary of a keyboard that has no physical keys, but you will be pleasantly surprised at how well it works.

Some applications automatically show the keyboard when you need to enter text. If the keyboard does not appear, touch the area where you want to type and the keyboard slides up ready for use.

Touch to capitalize the next character

Touch for numbers and symbols

Double-tap to engage CAPS Lock

Touch to speak the text   **Touch to hide the keyboard**

Keyboard Quick Tips

If you are typing an email address or a website address, the keyboard shows a button labeled .COM. If you touch it, you type .COM but if you touch and hold it, you can choose between .EDU, .GOV, .ORG, and .NET. If you touch and hold the Return key, the cursor jumps to the next field. This is useful if you are filling out forms on a website or moving between fields in an app. If you touch and hold the microphone key, the input options and keyboard settings change.

Using the virtual keyboard as you type, your Google Nexus Tablet makes word suggestions. Think of this as similar to the spell checker you would see in a word processor. Your Google Nexus Tablet uses a dictionary of words to guess what you are typing. If the word you were going to type is highlighted, touch space or period to select it. If you can see the word in the list but it is not highlighted, touch the word to select it.

List of suggested words

Touch to select an alternative suggested word

Touch space to accept the suggested word in the middle

Add Your Word

If you type a word that you know is correct, you can add it to your personal dictionary so that next time you type it, your Google Nexus Tablet won't try to correct it. To do this, after you have typed the word, you see it as the middle suggested word. Touch the word once. Your word is underlined in red and listed in the suggested words area. Touch it one more time to add it to your personal dictionary.

Touch to add your word to the dictionary

Touch your word again to complete the save

To make the next letter you type a capital letter, touch the Shift key. To make all letters capitals (or CAPS), double-tap the Shift key to engage CAPS Lock. Touch Shift again to disengage CAPS Lock.

To type numbers or symbols, touch the Symbols key.

When on the Numbers and Symbols screen, touch the Symbols key to see extra symbols. Touch the ABC key to return to the regular keyboard.

To enter an accented character, touch and hold any vowel or the C, N, or S keys. A small window opens enabling you to select an accented or alternative character. Slide your finger over the accented character and lift your finger to type it.

Touch to return to letters

Touch to see more symbols

**Touch and hold
for accented
characters**

To reveal other alternative characters, touch and hold any other letter, number, or symbol.

Want a Larger Keyboard?

Turn your Google Nexus Tablet sideways to switch to a landscape keyboard. The landscape keyboard has larger keys and is easier to type on.

**Landscape
keyboard**

Gesture Typing: Swipe to Type

Your Google Nexus Tablet's keyboard supports regular typing and swiping to type. To use this feature anytime, simply swipe your finger over all the letters in a word you want to type. As you swipe, you'll see a blue trail following your finger. For words with double letters, loop around the letter to type it twice. Don't worry about spaces, as they'll be inserted for you.

Dictation: Speak Instead of Typing

Your Google Nexus Tablet can turn your voice into text. It uses Google's speech recognition service, which means that you must have a connection to the cellular network or a Wi-Fi network in order to use it.

Touch to select a different dictation language

1. Touch the microphone key.

2. Wait until you see "Speak now "and then start saying what you want to be typed. You can speak the punctuation by saying "comma," "question mark," "exclamation mark," or "exclamation point."

3. Stop speaking to finish dictation.

Touch to cancel voice dictation

Editing Text

After you enter text, you can edit it by cutting, copying, or pasting the text. Here is how to select and copy text and then paste over a word with the copied text.

1. While you are typing, touch and hold a word you want to copy.

2. Slide the blue end markers until you have selected all of the text you want to copy.

3. Touch to copy the text.

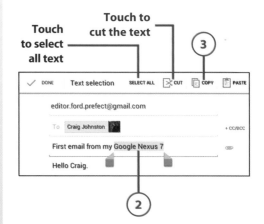

4. Touch and hold the word you want to paste over.

5. Touch Paste.

Simpler Copy/Paste

You might want to just copy some text and paste it somewhere else, instead of pasting it over a word. To do this, after you have copied the text, touch once in the text area, move the single blue marker to where you want to paste the text. Touch the blue marker again and touch Paste.

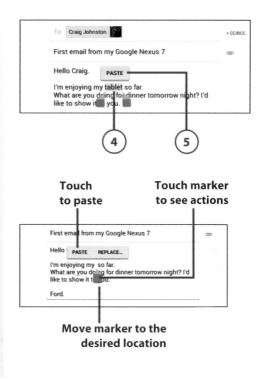

Touch to paste **Touch marker to see actions**

Move marker to the desired location

Menus

Your Google Nexus Tablet has two types of menus: Regular menus and Context menus. Let's go over what each one does.

Most applications have a Menu button (menu). These enable you to make changes or take actions within that application. The Menu button should always appear in the top-right of an app, however it can sometimes appear in the System Bar next to the Recent Apps button, or elsewhere in the app.

Touch the Menu button to reveal the App menu

A Context menu applies to an item on the screen. If you touch and hold something on the screen (in this example, a link on a web page), a Context menu appears. The items on the Context menu differ based on the type of object you touched.

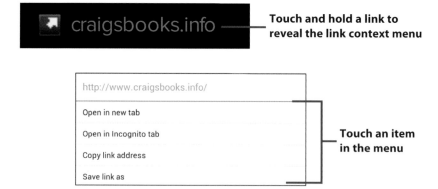

Touch and hold a link to reveal the link context menu

Touch an item in the menu

Switching Between Apps

As discussed earlier in this chapter, your Google Nexus Tablet has a new button called the Recent Apps button. This button is always in the System Bar at the bottom of your screen. You can use this button to switch between apps, close apps, and force them to quit if they have stopped responding. Here is how.

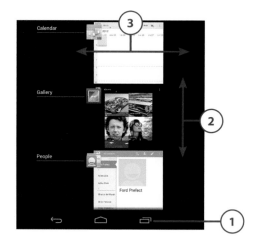

1. Touch the Recent Apps button.

2. Scroll up and down the list of recent apps.

3. Swipe an app left or right off the screen to close it.

4. Touch and hold an app to reveal the menu.

5. Touch to force an app to close and see more information about the app.

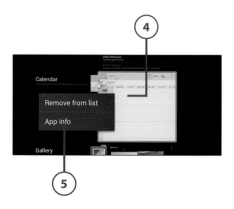

Installing Synchronization Software

Because your Google Nexus Tablet is tightly integrated with Google and its services, all media that you purchase on your tablet is stored in the Google cloud and accessible anywhere and anytime. However, you might have a lot of music on your computer already that you need to copy to your Google cloud and so you need to install the Google Music Manager software or the Android File Transfer app for your Mac to copy any file back and forth.

Installing Android File Transfer (Apple Mac OSX)

You only need the Android File Transfer app when using a Samsung Android tablet (such as your Google Nexus Tablet) on an Apple Mac running OS X.

1. From your Mac, browse to http://www.android.com /filetransfer/ and download the Android File Transfer app.

2. Click the downloads icon to reveal your downloaded files.

3. Double-click androidfiletransfer. dmg in your Safari Downloads.

4. Drag the green Android to the Applications shortcut to install the app.

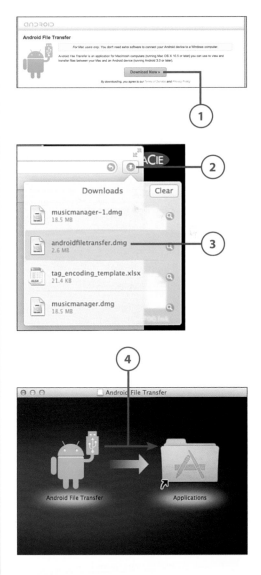

Installing Google Music Manager (Apple Mac)

Don't install Google Music Manager unless you plan to upload files from your computer to the Google Music cloud.

1. Visit https://play.google.com/music/listen#manager_pl from your desktop web browser and log in to your Google account if prompted.

2. Click to download Music Manager.

3. Click the downloads icon to reveal your downloaded files.

4. Double-click musicmanager.dmg in your Safari Downloads.

5. Drag the Music Manager icon to the Applications shortcut to install the app.

6. Double-click the Music Manager icon in the Applications folder.

7. Skip to the "Configuring Music Manager" sections later in the chapter to complete the installation.

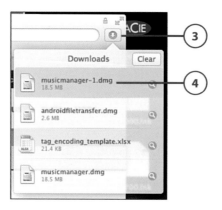

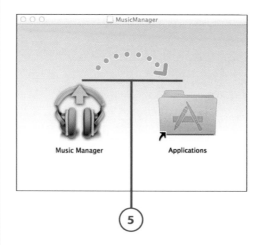

Installing Google Music Manager (Windows)

Don't install Google Music Manager unless you plan to upload files from your computer to the Google Music cloud.

1. Visit https://music.google.com/ music/listen#manager_pl from your desktop web browser and log in to your Google account if prompted.

2. Click to download Music Manager.

3. Double-click the musicmanagerinstaller app in your Downloads folder.

4. Skip to the "Configuring Music Manager" sections later in the chapter to complete the installation.

Configuring Music Manager (Windows and Apple Mac)

1. Click Continue.

2. Enter your Google (Gmail) email address.

3. Enter your Google (Gmail) password.

4. Click Continue.

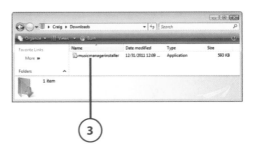

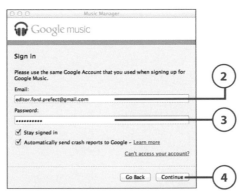

5. Choose where you keep your music.

6. Click Continue.

7. Choose whether to upload all of your music or just some of your playlists. Remember that you can only upload 20,000 songs for free. Skip to Step 12 if you choose to upload all music.

8. Check if you want to also upload podcasts.

9. Click Continue.

10. Select one or more playlists of music.

11. Click Continue.

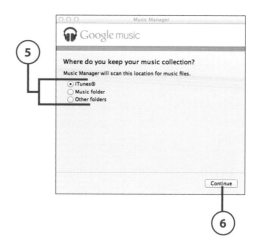

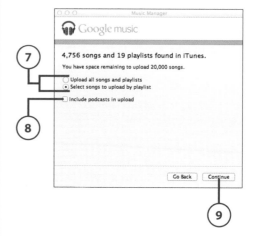

12. Choose whether you want to automatically upload any new music that is added to your computer.

13. Click Continue.

14. Click Close.

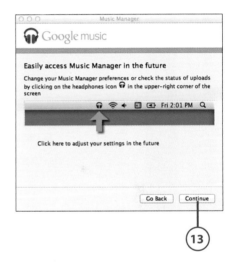

Choose what to show

Edit a contact

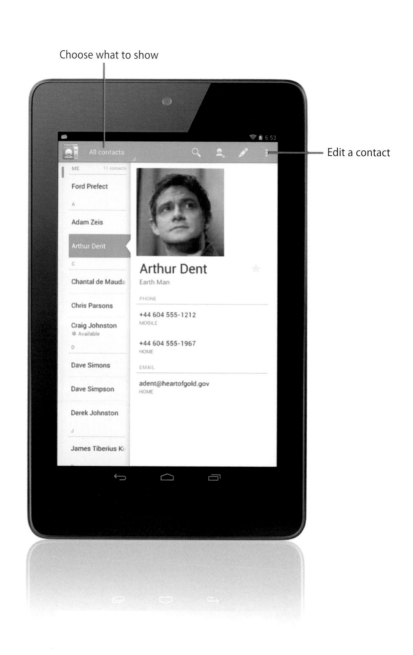

In this chapter, you discover the app that's your Google Nexus Tablet's hub of all communication, People. You learn how to add contacts, synchronize contacts, join duplicate contacts together, and even how to add a contact to your Home screen. Topics include the following:

→ Importing contacts

→ Adding contacts

→ Synchronizing contacts

→ Creating favorite contacts

People (Contacts)

On the Google Nexus Tablet, the Contacts app is called People. You can synchronize your contacts from many online sites such as Facebook and Gmail, so as your friends change their Facebook profile pictures, their pictures on your Google Nexus Tablet change, too.

Adding Accounts

Before you look around the People application, try adding some accounts to synchronize contacts from. You already added your Google account when you set up your Google Nexus Tablet in the "Prologue."

Adding Facebook, Twitter, LinkedIn, and Other Accounts

To add accounts for your online services such as Facebook, Twitter, LinkedIn, and so on, install the apps for those services from Google Play. Please see how to install apps in Chapter 8, "Working with Android Applications." After they are installed and you have logged into them, if you visit the Accounts section in Settings and add a new account as shown in the following sections, you will see new accounts for each online service.

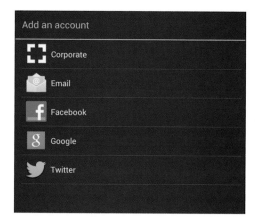

Adding a Work Email Account

Your Google Nexus Tablet can synchronize your contacts from your work email account as long as your company uses Microsoft Exchange or an email gateway that supports Microsoft ActiveSync (such as Lotus Traveler for Lotus Domino/ Notes email systems). It might be useful to be able to keep your work and personal contacts on one mobile device.

1. From the Home screen, pull down the Quick Setting Bar.

2. Touch the Settings icon.

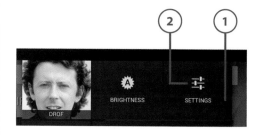

3. Scroll down until you see the Accounts section and touch Add Account.

4. Touch Corporate.

5. Enter your full corporate email address.

6. Enter your corporate network password.

7. Touch Next.

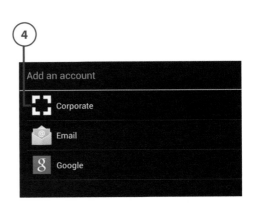

Error Adding Account? Guess the Server

Your Google Nexus Tablet tries to work out some information about your company's ActiveSync setup. If it can't, you are prompted to enter the ActiveSync server name manually. If you don't know what it is, you can try guessing it. If, for example, your email address is dsimons@allhitradio.com, the ActiveSync server is most probably webmail.allhitradio.com. If this doesn't work, ask your email administrator.

8. Enter your company's mail server name.

9. Touch to use secure connections, which encrypts your email, calendar, and contacts between your Google Nexus Tablet and your company's mail server. It is highly recommended that you leave this selected.

10. Touch to accept all encryption certificates without validating them. It is not advisable to check this box because you could become the victim of hacking.

11. Touch Next.

12. Touch to agree that your mail administrator might impose security restrictions on your Google Nexus Tablet if you proceed.

Remote Security Administration

Remote Security Administration is another way of saying that when you activate your Google Nexus Tablet against your work email servers, your email administrator can add restrictions to your tablet. The restrictions can include forcing a lock screen password, imposing the need for a very strong password, and requiring how many letters and numbers the password must be. Your email administrator also has the power to remotely wipe your Google Nexus Tablet so that it is put back to factory defaults, which is what the administrator might do if you lose your tablet or it is stolen.

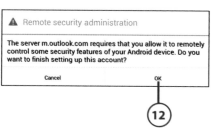

13. Touch to choose how often your corporate email is delivered to your Google Nexus Tablet. Automatic means that as it arrives in your Inbox at work, it is delivered to your tablet. You can set it to Manual, which means that your work email is only delivered when you open the Email app on your tablet. You can also set the delivery frequency from every 5 minutes to every hour.

14. Touch to choose how many days in the past email is synchronized to your Google Nexus Tablet or set it to All to synchronize all email in your Inbox.

15. Touch to enable or disable sending email from your Google Nexus Tablet using your corporate email account by default. When enabled, any time you choose to compose a new email, your corporate account is used.

16. Touch to enable or disable being notified when new email arrives from your corporate Inbox.

17. Touch to enable or disable synchronizing your corporate contacts to your Google Nexus Tablet.

18. Touch to enable or disable synchronizing your corporate calendar to your Google Nexus Tablet.

19. Touch to enable or disable synchronizing your corporate email to your Google Nexus Tablet.

20. Touch to enable or disable automatically downloading email attachments when your Google Nexus Tablet is connected to a Wi-Fi network.

21. Touch Next.

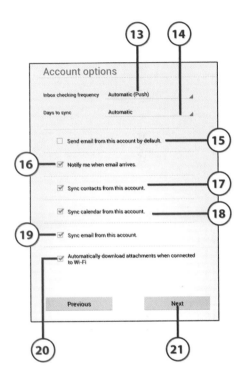

What to Synchronize

You might decide that you don't want to synchronize all your work information to your Google Nexus Tablet. You might decide to just synchronize email, and not the calendar, or maybe just the calendar but not the contacts and email. Unchecking these boxes enables you to choose the information you don't want to synchronize.

22. Enter a name for this email account. Use something meaningful that describes the purpose of the account such as "Work Email."

23. Touch Next.

24. Touch Activate.

Remove an Account

To remove an account, under the Accounts section in Settings, touch the account to be removed. For account types that can have multiple accounts (like Corporate and Google), touch the account again on the next screen to show its sync settings. Touch the Menu button on the top right of the screen and touch Remove Account.

Navigating People

The People app actually has three screens. The middle one you see shows you your list of contacts, but there are two others that have specific functions.

1. From the Home screen, touch the People icon.

2. Touch to add a new contact.

3. Touch to search for a contact.

4. Touch the Menu button to change the settings for the People app, manage accounts, import or export contacts, delete the selected contact, and choose which contacts to display.

5. Touch a contact to see all information about him.

6. Touch to change what contacts to display. You can choose All contacts, Favorite contacts, or Groups.

7. Touch to edit the current contact.

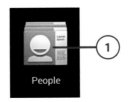

People

Indicates a contact's
Google Talk status

Mark a Contact As Favorite

To mark a contact as a favorite, while you have the contact's information open, touch the star icon next to their name.

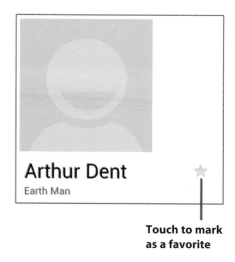

Arthur Dent
Earth Man

Touch to mark as a favorite

Its Not All Good

Social Networking Status Updates and Syncing Not Working

Because of a dispute between Google and Facebook and Twitter, all of the social networking synchronization and status updates do not currently work. You can work-around this issue for Facebook only by installing an app called HaxSync. Status updates from other apps like Skype will be displayed however.

Editing a Contact

Sometimes you need to make changes to a contact or add additional information to it.

1. Touch the contact to edit.

2. Touch the Edit button.

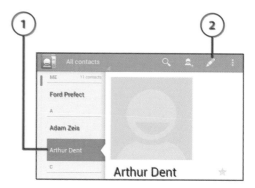

3. Touch to enter a middle name, name prefix, and name suffix.

4. Touch an X next to a field to delete it.

5. Touch to change the field subcategory. In this example, touching Mobile enables you to change the subcategory from Mobile to Home.

6. Touch Add New to add a new field in a specific category. In this example, touching Add New enables you to add a new phone number.

7. Touch to put the contact in a contact group. You can use a default contact group of family, friends, co-workers, or you can create a group.

8. Touch to add a new field to the contact's contact card. New fields could be IM (Instant Messaging), Notes, Nickname, website, an event (like a birthday or anniversary), and even an Internet phone contact (or Voice over IP number).

9. Touch Done to save your changes.

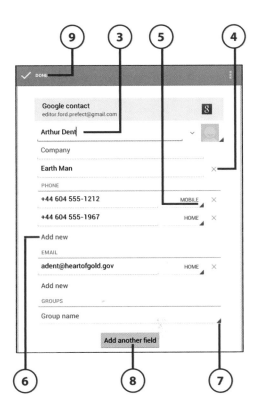

You Don't Need to Add Google Talk

If your contact has a Gmail email address, the People app automatically adds a Google Talk (GTalk) IM field for them, but it is hidden.

Adding a Contact Photo

The contact photo is normally added automatically when a social network account is linked to a contact. However, due to the fact that this functionality is not working right now (see the earlier It's Not All Good sidebar on social networking updates), you can manually add a picture.

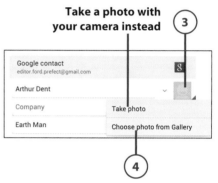

(1) **(2)**

1. Touch the Contact.

2. Touch the Edit button.

3. Touch the contact photo placeholder.

4. Touch to add a photo already saved on your Google Nexus Tablet.

5. Touch the album where the photo is located.

6. Touch the photo.

Take a photo with your camera instead **(3)**

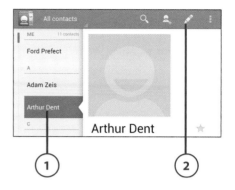

(4)

(5)

(6)

7. Drag the cropping box to select the area of the photo you want to use as the contact photo.

8. Drag the outside of the cropping box to expand or contract it.

9. Touch OK to save the cropped photo as the contact photo.

10. Touch Done to save the changes to the contact card.

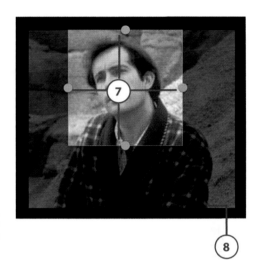

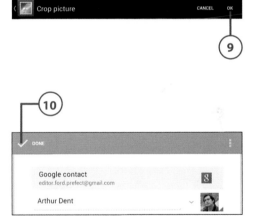

Adding and Managing Contacts

As you add contacts to your work email account or Google account, those contacts are synchronized to your Google Nexus Tablet automatically. When you reply to or forward emails on your tablet to an email address that is not in your Contacts, those email addresses are automatically added to the contact list or merged into an existing contact with the same name. You can also add contacts to your Google Nexus Tablet directly.

Adding Contacts from an Email

To manually add a contact from an email, first open the email client (either email or Gmail) and then open an email message. Please see Chapter 4, "Email," for more on how to work with email.

1. Touch the blank contact picture to the left of the sender's name.

2. Touch the larger blank contact picture that pops up.

3. Touch to add the sender's email address to your contacts.

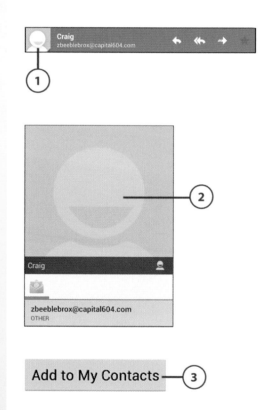

Adding a Contact Manually

1. Touch the People icon on the Home screen.

2. Touch to add a new contact.

3. Touch to select which account the new contact is being added to. For example you might want to add the new contact to your work email account instead of your personal account.

4. Enter the person's full name including any middle name. Your Google Nexus Tablet automatically populates the first name, middle name, and last name fields.

5. Touch to choose a contact picture.

6. Touch to enter a middle name, name prefix and suffix, and phonetic names.

7. Enter information including phone numbers, email address, and events.

8. Touch to add a new field to the contact's contact card. New fields could be IM (Instant Messaging), Notes, Nickname, website, an event (like a birthday or anniversary), and even an Internet phone contact (or Voice over IP number).

9. Touch to put the contact in a contact group. You can use a default contact group such as family, friends, or co-workers, or you can create a group.

10. Touch Done to save the new contact.

People

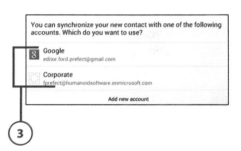

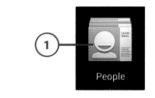

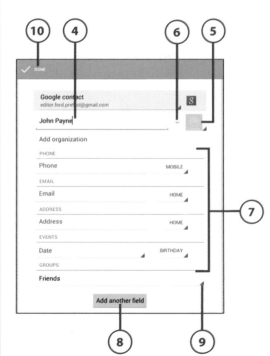

Adding a Contact from a vCard

vCards are files that can be attached to emails. These vCards contain a virtual business card that you can import into the People app as a new contact. Use the following steps to save a vCard to your Google Nexus Tablet.

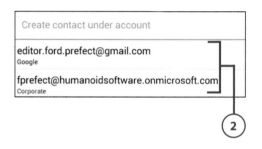

1. Touch View under the attachment that has the .vcf extension.

2. Touch to select which account you want to add the new contact to. For example you might want to add the new contact to your work email account instead of your personal account.

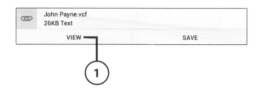

Adding a Contact Using Near Field Communications

Your Google Nexus Tablet has Near Field Communications (NFC) functionality built in. This enables you to exchange contact cards between NFC-enabled smartphones and tablets or to purchase items in a store by just holding your Google Nexus Tablet near the NFC reader at the check-out counter. If you encounter someone who has an NFC-enabled smartphone or tablet, or she has an NFC tag that contains her business card, follow these steps to import that information.

1. Hold the other person's smartphone or tablet back to back with your Google Nexus Tablet, or hold the NFC tag close to the back cover of your tablet. Your Google Nexus Tablet's screen dims and it plays a tone to indicate that it is reading the NFC information.

2. Touch to select which account you want to add the new contact to. For example you might want to add the new contact to your work email account instead of your personal account.

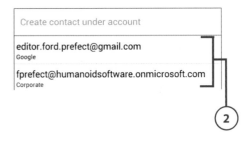

More About NFC

Your Google Nexus Tablet has an NFC radio and antenna built-in. When you hold either another smartphone or tablet with NFC or an NFC tag close to the back cover, the NFC antenna and radio read the data. See more about your Google Nexus Tablet's NFC antenna at http://www.ifixit.com/Teardown/Nexus-7-Teardown/9623/1, and read more about NFC at http://en.wikipedia.org/wiki/Near_field_communication.

Beam a Contact

If you want to send a contact via NFC, you can use a feature built into your Google Nexus tablet called Beaming. To beam a contact, make sure the contact is selected and bring the other person's NFC-enabled smartphone or tablet back to back with your tablet. After you hear a tone, you see the screen zoom out. Touch the screen to send the contact card.

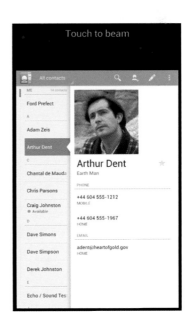

People Settings

There are a couple of settings that you might want to customize for the People app, such as choosing the contact list display order and whether to display contacts using their first names first or last names first.

1. Touch the Menu button.

2. Touch Settings.

3. Touch to choose the sort order of the list of contacts in the People app. You can sort the list by first name or last name.

4. Touch to choose how each contact is displayed. You can display contacts as first name first or last name first.

5. Touch to save the settings.

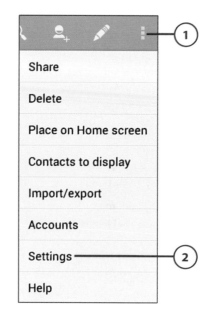

Creating Contact Groups

You can create contact groups—such as Friends, Family, Inner Circle—and then divide your contacts among them. This can be useful if you don't want to search through all your contacts to find a family member. Instead you can just touch the Family group and see only family members.

1. Touch All Contacts.

2. Touch Groups.

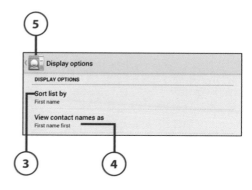

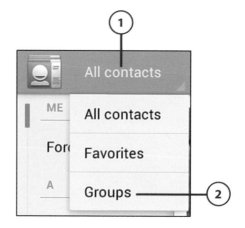

3. Touch to create a new group.

4. Touch the account where you want to create the new group.

5. Enter a name for your new group.

6. Start typing the name of a contact to add to the group. Your Google Nexus Tablet displays names that match what you are typing.

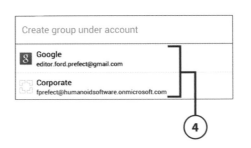

7. Touch the name from the list of matches to add that person to the new group.

8. Repeat Steps 5 and 6 to add more people to the group.

9. Touch Done to save the group.

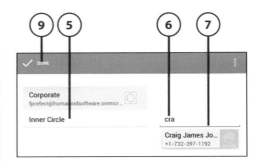

Editing Contact Groups

1. Touch All Contacts.

2. Touch Groups.

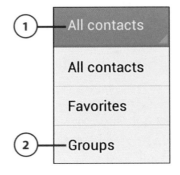

3. Touch the group to edit.

4. Touch the Edit button.

5. Touch to change the name of the group. Note that some Google groups cannot be renamed.

6. Enter a name to add an extra person to the group.

7. Touch the X icon next to a contact to remove them from the group.

8. Touch Done to save the group.

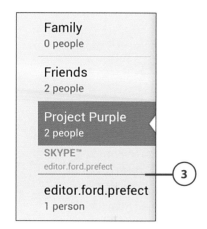

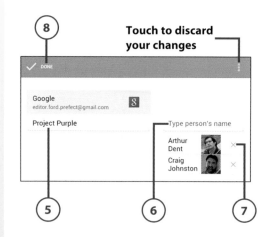

Touch to discard your changes

Choosing Contacts To Display

You can choose to hide certain contact groups from the main contacts display; for example, you can choose to show only contacts from Twitter. You can also choose which contact groups in each account to include.

1. Touch the Menu button.

2. Touch Contacts to Display.

3. Touch to show all contacts from all accounts.

4. Touch an account to show only contacts in that account.

5. Touch to customize which groups in each account are displayed.

6. Touch to expand an account to see subgroups of contacts.

7. Touch to select or deselect a subgroup of contacts.

8. Touch OK to save the settings.

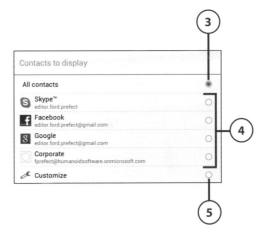

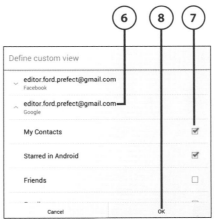

Joining and Separating Contacts

As you add contacts to your Google Nexus Tablet, they are automatically merged if the new contact name matches a name that's already stored. Sometimes you need to manually join contacts together or separate them if your Google Nexus Tablet has joined them in error.

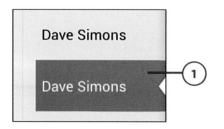

Joining Contacts Manually

1. Touch the contact that you want to join a contact to.

2. Touch the Edit button.

3. Touch the Menu button.

4. Touch Join.

5. Touch the contact you want to join with.

6. Touch Done to complete the join process.

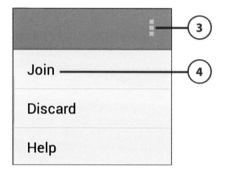

Separating Contacts

1. Touch the contact that you want to separate.

2. Touch the Edit button.

3. Touch the Menu button.

4. Touch Separate.

5. Touch OK to separate the contacts.

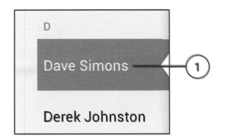

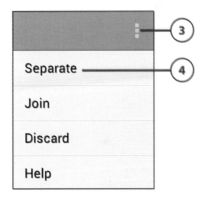

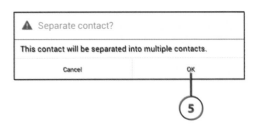

Adding a Contact to Your Home Screen

If you communicate with some contacts so much that you are constantly opening and closing the People application, a quicker solution might be to add a shortcut to the contacts on the Home screen.

1. Touch the contact you want to add to your Home screen.

2. Touch the Menu button.

3. Touch Place on Home Screen. A shortcut to the contact is placed on an available spot on the Home screen.

Reposition or Remove the Shortcut

After you have a contact shortcut on your Home screen, you can reposition it by touching and holding it, and while you are still holding it, drag it around the screen, or off the sides of the screen to move it between the Home screens. Release the shortcut to complete the reposition. To remove the contact shortcut, touch and hold it, then drag it up to where you see the word Remove and release it.

Drag it around to reposition it

IMPORTING AND EXPORTING CONTACTS

>>Go Further

You can import any vCards that you have saved to your Google Nexus Tablet's internal storage. You can also export your entire contact list to your Google Nexus Tablet's internal storage or share that entire contact list via Bluetooth, email, Gmail, or, if you have any NFC tag writer software installed, write it to an NFC tag. To access the import/export functions, touch the Menu button and touch Import/Export. When you export contacts to storage, you can find them in /mnt/sdcard when browsing your Google Nexus Tablet from your Mac or PC.

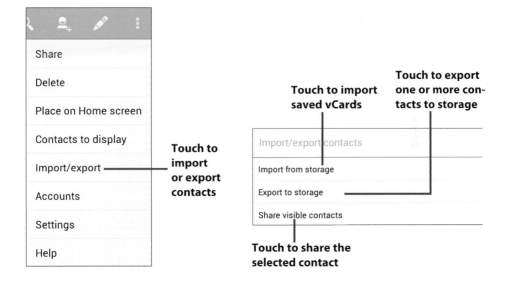

Share

Delete

Place on Home screen

Contacts to display

Import/export ———— **Touch to import or export contacts**

Accounts

Settings

Help

Touch to import saved vCards

Touch to export one or more contacts to storage

Import/export contacts

Import from storage

Export to storage

Share visible contacts

Touch to share the selected contact

Touch to
find movies

Touch to
find TV shows

In this chapter, you discover your Google Nexus Tablet's audio and video capabilities, including how your Google Nexus Tablet plays video and music, and how you can synchronize audio and video from your desktop computer or Google Play Music. Topics include the following:

➜ Using Google Play Music for music
➜ Using the Gallery application for pictures and video
➜ Renting movies with Google Play
➜ Working with YouTube

Audio, Video, and Movies

Your Google Nexus Tablet has strong multimedia abilities. The large screen enables you to turn your Google Nexus Tablet sideways to enjoy a video in its original 16:9 ratio. You can also use your Google Nexus Tablet to search YouTube, watch videos, and even upload videos to YouTube right from your tablet. Android version 4.1 fully embraces the cloud, which enables you to store your music collection on Google's servers so you can access it anywhere.

Music

Your Google Nexus Tablet ships with an app called Google Play Music, which enables you to listen to music stored on your tablet as well as from your collection in the Google Play Music cloud. Using Google Play you can also find and buy more music.

Finding Music

The best place to discover and find music is in the Google Play store.

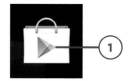

1. Touch the Google Play icon on the Home screen.

2. Touch to see only music.

3. Touch to launch the Google Play Music app.

4. Touch to change the settings for Google Play.

5. Scroll down to see all featured music.

6. Swipe left to see a list of music Genres.

7. Swipe right to see the Top Albums and Top Songs.

8. Touch to search for music.

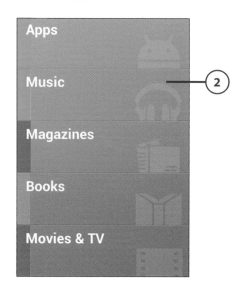

Purchasing Music

After you find a song or album you want to purchase follow these steps.

Free Music

Sometimes songs are offered for free. If a song is offered for free you see the word FREE instead of a price for the song. Even though the song is free, you still need to follow the steps outlined in this section; however, the price is reflected as 0.

1. Touch the price to the right of the song title or album.

2. Touch Accept & Buy.

3. Touch Listen to hear your song after the purchase is complete. The song opens in the Play Music app.

Touch to play a preview of the song before purchasing it

Touch to change your method of payment

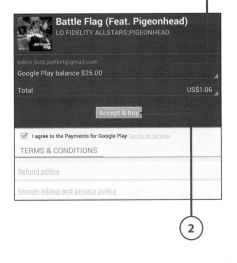

Its Not All Good

Cloud and Data Usage

Although the idea of cloud storage (where your music is stored on Google computers as opposed to your Google Nexus Tablet) is very beneficial, it does mean that anytime you listen to your music collection it is streamed over the Wi-Fi network. If you are not connected to Wi-Fi you are unable to access and listen to your music. You can plan for a no-coverage situation by keeping some music on your tablet. See the section titled "Listening to Music with No Wireless Coverage" later in this chapter.

Adding Your Existing Music to Google Play Music

You can upload as many as 20,000 songs from Apple iTunes, Microsoft Windows Media Player, or music stored in folders on your computer for free to your Google Play Music cloud account by using the Google Music Manager app on your desktop computer. If you haven't already installed Google Music Manager, please follow the steps in the "Installing Google Music Manager" sections in the Prologue.

1. Click (right-click for Windows) the Google Music Manager icon. (This icon is in the Mac Menu Bar at the top of the screen or in the Windows Task Bar at the bottom of the screen.)

2. Choose Preferences. (Use the Options command if you are on Windows.)

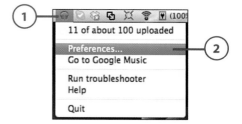

3. Click to upload new songs that have been added since you last used Music Manager to upload music.

4. Click to upload the remainder of songs that have not yet uploaded.

5. Click to upload songs in certain playlists. This only works for iTunes or for Windows Media Player.

6. Choose the playlists to upload.

7. Click Upload after you have made your selections.

8. Click to allow Google Music Manager to automatically upload new songs added.

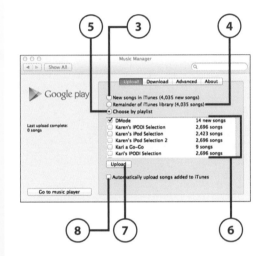

Automatic Upload

If you choose to have your music uploaded automatically in Step 8, Google Music Manager continually monitors Apple iTunes, Microsoft Windows Media Player, or your Music folders to see when you add music. If it finds new music, Google Music Manager automatically uploads it. (After you install Google Music Manager, the software is always running on your computer.)

What If I Don't Have iTunes or Windows Media Player?

If you don't have or don't use Apple iTunes or Microsoft Windows Media Player to store and play your music, Google Music Manager can upload music from folders on your computer. Click the Advanced Tab, click Change, and select either Music folder (to use the folder on your computer called Music) or Other folders (so you can choose folders where you store your music). Click Add Folder to add a new folder to the list.

Select to choose other folders

Can I Download Music to My Computer?

You can download your entire music collection from Google Play Music to your computer, or just download music you have purchased on your Google Nexus Tablet by clicking the Download tab in Google Music Manager Preferences.

Click to download your music

Using the Music Application

Now that you have purchased some music and synchronized it from your computer, it's time to take a look at the Google Play Music app on your Google Nexus Tablet.

1. Touch the Play Music icon on the Home screen.

Play Music

①

Swipe Between Views

As you follow the steps in this task, instead of touching the view titles such as Albums and Artists, you can swipe left and right to move between these views instead.

Accessing Filter Views on the Nexus 10

On the Nexus 10 tablet, the main Music screen is a cover flow and you cannot swipe left and right to change the filter view. Instead touch Recent on the top-left to choose the filter.

Touch to filter the view

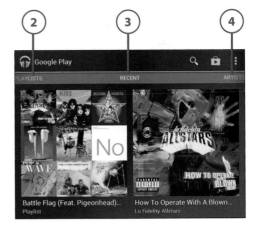

Swipe through the music

2. Touch Playlists to show any music playlists that you have synchronized to your Google Nexus Tablet. Find out more about how to do that later in the chapter.

3. Touch Recent to see recently played songs, mixes, or albums.

4. Touch Artists to filter the view by artist. Touch an artist's name to reveal songs by that artist and then touch a song to play it.

5. Touch Albums to filter the view by album title. Touch an album name to reveal songs on that album and then touch a song to play it.

6. Touch Songs to filter the view by song title. This shows all songs by all artists. Touch a song to play it.

7. Touch Genres to filter the view by genre. Touch an album name to reveal songs on that album and then touch a song to play it.

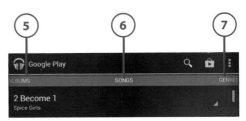

8. Touch to get music from the Google Play store.

9. Touch to search for music in your collection.

What's Playing

If you are currently playing music, the bottom of the Music app shows the information about the song and allows you to pause it, or jump backwards and forwards through the playlist.

What's currently playing

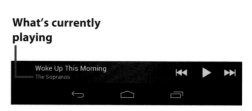

Controlling Playback

While your music is playing, you have some control over how a song plays and the selection of music that plays.

1. Touch to jump to the previous song in the album, playlist, or shuffle.

2. Touch to jump to the next song in the album, playlist, or shuffle.

3. Touch to pause the song. The button turns into the play button when a song is paused. Touch again to resume playing a paused song.

4. Touch to see the list of songs.

5. Touch anywhere on the screen to reveal the shuffle and repeat icons.

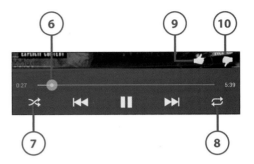

6. Drag to skip forward and backward through the song.

7. Touch to enable or disable song shuffling. When Shuffle is enabled, songs in the current playlist, album, or song list are randomly played.

8. Touch to enable repeating. Touch once to repeat all songs; touch again to repeat the current song only; touch again to disable repeating.

9. Touch to indicate that you like the song. The Google Play Music app adds the song to the "Thumbs up" playlist.

10. Touch to indicate that you do not like the song.

11. Touch to see more options.

12. Touch to make an instant mix based on the song or shop for more songs by the artist.

13. Touch to clear the queue of songs you made earlier and stop playing the current song. If you didn't make a queue, the current song stops playing.

14. Touch to create a playlist and add the current song to it.

15. Touch to change the Play Music app settings.

16. Touch to use the graphic equalizer to adjust the way your music sounds.

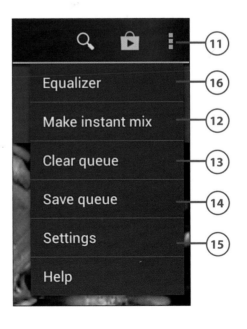

What Is an Instant Mix?

If you are playing a song and choose to create an Instant Mix as mentioned in Step 12, the Google Play Music app creates a new playlist and adds songs to it that are similar to the one you are currently playing. The name of the playlist is the name of the current song plus the word mix. For example if you are playing the song "Galvanize" and choose to create an Instant Mix, the playlist is called "Galvanize Mix."

No repeating

Repeat all songs

Repeat current song

What Is the Queue?

As you see in Step 13, you can clear the queue, but what is the queue? Essentially the queue is the Now Playing queue, a dynamic playlist that you can add songs to so that they are queued up to play one after the other. To add music to the queue, touch and hold a song, playlist, or album and choose Add to Queue.

Adjust the Equalizer

The Google Play Music app has a Graphic Equalizer that enables you to select pre-set audio configurations or use your own. While a song is playing, use the following steps to use or adjust the Equalizer.

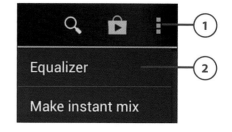

1. Touch the Menu button.

2. Touch Equalizer.

3. Touch to turn the Equalizer on and off.

4. Touch to select from a list of preset Equalizer settings such as Dance, Hip Hop, and many more.

5. Drag the frequency response sliders to enhance or deemphasize certain frequencies.

6. Drag the slider to adjust the bass boost.

7. Drag the slider to adjust the 3D effect, which helps the music sound like it's all around as opposed to just in your two ears.

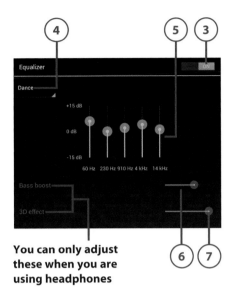

You can only adjust these when you are using headphones

Work and Listen to Music

You don't have to keep the Google Play Music app open while you are playing music, you can switch back to the Home screen and run any other app but still have the ability to control the music.

1. Pull down the Notification Bar.

2. Touch to pause the song.

3. Touch to jump to the next song in the list, album, or playlist.

4. Touch the song title to open the Google Play Music app for more control.

5. Touch to stop playing the song and remove the playback control from the Notification Bar.

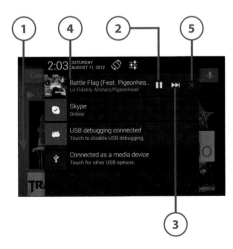

Control Music from the Lock Screen

Even if your tablet is locked, you can control music playback without having to first unlock it. When you press the Power button, the music playback controls appear on the lock screen.

Managing Playlists

Playlists enable you to group songs together. Here is how to create them and use them.

Creating a New Playlist on Your Google Nexus Tablet

1. Touch the Menu button while viewing the Playlists view.

2. Touch New playlist.

3. Enter a name for your new playlist.

4. Touch OK.

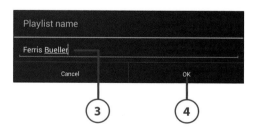

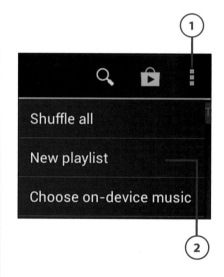

Adding a Song to an Existing Playlist

1. Touch and hold on a song.

2. Touch Add to Playlist.

3. Touch the name of the playlist you want to add the song to.

Rearranging Songs in a Playlist

1. Touch a playlist to show the songs in it.

2. Touch and hold the symbol to the left of a song you want to move. Move that song up and down until it is in the right place, and then release it.

Delete or Rename a Playlist

1. Touch and hold on the playlist you want to delete or rename.

2. Touch to delete the playlist.

3. Touch to rename the playlist.

Listening to Music with No Wireless Coverage

As established earlier in the chapter, if you utilize Google Play Music to store your music in Google's cloud, when you play that music on your Google Nexus Tablet it is actually streaming over the Wi-Fi network. If you know that you are going to be in an area without Wi-Fi coverage but still want to listen to your music, follow these steps.

1. Touch the Menu button while viewing the Albums, Playlists, or Artists views.

2. Touch Choose On-Device Music to select music that must remain on your tablet.

3. Touch the push pins next to songs, artists, playlists, or albums that you want to keep on your tablet.

4. Touch the check mark to save your selection and start the music download to your Google Nexus Tablet.

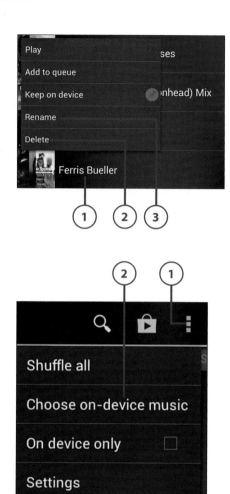

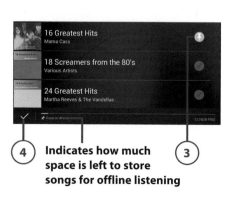

Indicates how much space is left to store songs for offline listening

Changing Google Play Music Settings

1. Touch the Menu button.

2. Touch to show only music you have directly copied to your tablet from a computer or chosen to be made available offline.

3. Touch Settings.

4. Touch to change the Google Account being used for Google Play Music.

5. Touch to show only music stored on your Google Nexus Tablet. When this setting is on you see only music you have directly copied to your tablet from a computer or chosen to be made available offline.

6. Touch to enable or disable caching of streamed music. When this is enabled, music you are listening to is temporarily stored on your Google Nexus Tablet so if you play one of the songs again, it plays it straight from memory.

7. Touch to enable or disable streaming high-quality music. When this option is enabled and you listen to music not already stored on your Google Nexus Tablet, the music streams at the highest quality.

8. Touch to manually refresh the list of music shown on your Google Nexus Tablet.

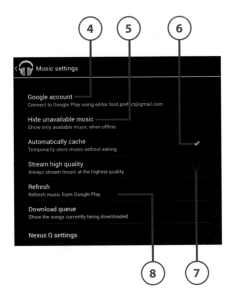

9. Touch to see the download queue. When you choose to make music available offline, that music is queued for download. You can see the download progress here.

10. Touch to download the Nexus Q app that enables you to play media on the Google Nexus Q media device.

11. Touch to save your changes.

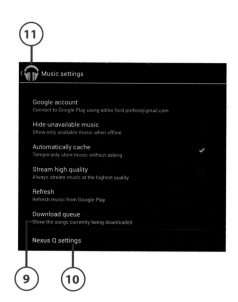

Nexus Q

The Nexus Q is a multimedia hub that connects to your television and enables you to play movies, TV shows, and music from the Google cloud. You can control the Nexus Q from your Google Nexus Tablet after you download the Nexus Q app mentioned in Step 10. As of the writing of this book, the Nexus Q has been pulled and cannot be purchased but this might change.

SYNCHRONIZE MUSIC AND OTHER MEDIA USING A CABLE

If for some reason you don't want to make use of Google Play Music or you can't because you live in a country where Google Play Music is not supported, you can synchronize music and other media using a cable (and sometimes over Wi-Fi). A great way to do this is to download an app called doubleTwist. doubleTwist has been providing media synchronization for many tablets for a while now, and the product is very mature. Head to http://doubleTwist.com to download the Windows or Mac version and then visit the Android Market to download the Android app companion.

BEAMING MUSIC BETWEEN ANDROID DEVICES

If you know someone with an Android smartphone or tablet that has an NFC chip, you should be able to beam music to them. In theory you should be able to send music to their device but as of the writing of this book, there seems to be a glitch preventing this from working correctly. If this feature is fixed in the future, you need to find the song you want to send and then hold your Google Nexus Tablet back to back with the other Android device. You'll hear a sound and the screen will also zoom out. Touch the screen to send the file. You can also send a link to a song in Google Play. To do that, find the song or album in the Google Play store. Touch your Google Nexus Tablet back to back with the other device. The screen will zoom out and you will hear a sound. Touch the screen to send the link. The other person's device will automatically open Google Play and show the song or album.

Touch to beam the song

Videos

Your Google Nexus 7 tablet does not have a rear-facing camera, and it does not have a camera app. This means that you cannot really use your tablet for taking pictures or recording video. The front-facing camera is really only meant for video chatting and unlocking your tablet using facial recognition. If you have a Nexus 10, which does have a rear-facing camera, please turn to Chapter 13 to read more about taking pictures and recording videos.

IS THERE A WAY TO STILL USE THE NEXUS 7 CAMERA APP?

>>>Go Further

Even though your Nexus 7 tablet doesn't come with a Camera app visible, it is actually still loaded but is kept hidden. To make it visible, search for an app in Google Play called "Camera Launcher For Nexus 7" by a developer called MODACO. Once installed, the app provides a link to the Camera app. However, remember that the app will be quite awkward to use because you can only use the front-facing camera, which makes taking any kind of photos or video very clumsy. If you choose to use this app and want some help with the Camera app, please look for my previous book called *My Samsung Galaxy Nexus* which covers the Camera app in detail.

Playing Videos

Even though there is no Camera app on your Google Nexus Tablet, you still have the ability to receive videos from your friends, or copy them onto your tablet from your computer (see the section titled "Copying Videos from Your Computer" later in this chapter). If you do have personal videos on your tablet, here is how to find them and play them.

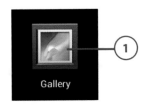

Gallery

1. Touch the Gallery icon to launch the Gallery application.

Indicates videos

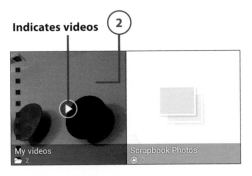

My videos
2

Scrapbook Photos
0

2. Touch an album to open it. Albums with videos have a little Play icon on their thumbnail.

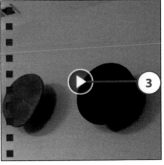

3. Touch a video to start playing it. Videos have a little Play icon on them.

4. Touch the screen while the video is playing to reveal the video controls.

5. Touch to pause or unpause the video.

6. Drag the slider to quickly skip forward and backward.

7. Rotate your Google Nexus Tablet sideways to allow the video to fill the screen.

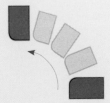

00:04   00:07

Sharing Videos

You can share small videos with people from the Gallery application.

1. Touch and hold the video you want to share.

2. Touch to share using a frequently used service, in this case Facebook.

3. Touch to see other ways to share the video.

4. Touch to send the video via Bluetooth.

5. Touch to send the video to Picasa.

6. Touch to send the video to Google+.

7. Touch to upload the video using other methods including YouTube, Email (not Gmail), Gmail, and Skype.

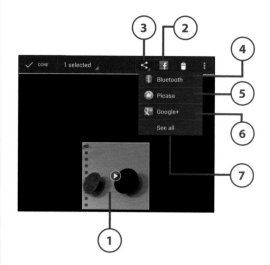

Bluetooth Sharing Might Fail

Many phones and tablets do not accept incoming Bluetooth files, but devices like computers do. Even on computers, the recipient must configure her Bluetooth configuration to accept incoming files.

Uploading or Sharing Multiple Videos

You can share or upload multiple videos at the same time, instead of one by one. After you touch and hold a video, touch more videos to add them to your list. When you select more than one video to share, however, the option to share on Facebook is disabled because you can only upload videos to Facebook one at a time. After you reduce your list of videos to share to only one video, the Facebook sharing option returns.

Deleting Videos

1. Touch and hold the video you want to delete.

2. Touch the trash icon to delete the video.

Delete Multiple Videos

You can delete multiple videos at the same time. To do this, after you touch and hold to select the first video, touch the other videos you want to delete. You see the number of select items increase in the upper-left corner of the screen. After you have chosen all the videos you want to delete, touch the trash icon to delete all of them at once.

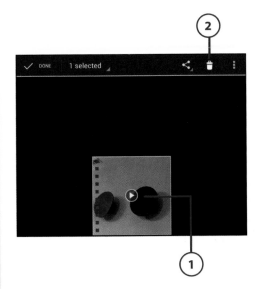

Gallery App Settings

1. Touch the Menu button.

2. Touch Settings.

3. Touch to edit the settings for your Google account, including turning Photo Sync on or off.

4. Touch to enable or disable synchronizing photos over Wi-Fi only. This setting is useless on your tablet because you can only connect via Wi-Fi and should always be left on.

5. Touch to save your changes.

What Is Photo Sync?

Photo Sync is a feature that automatically copies all photos you have uploaded from your computer to your Picasa web albums or have uploaded to your Google+ account. If you suddenly upload a lot of photos this way, you might notice a dramatic decrease in battery life as your tablet downloads all the pictures, but under normal use battery life should not be compromised.

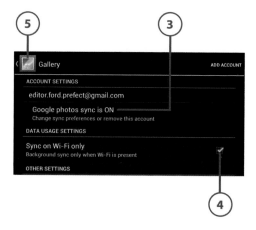

Movies and TV Shows

Google Play enables you to rent and purchase movies (mostly rent), and buy TV shows—even whole season passes of TV shows.

Buying and Renting Movies

As with music, when you buy or rent movies, they remain in the Google cloud and stream to your tablet when you want to watch them.

1. Touch to launch Google Play.

2. Touch Movies & TV.

3. Touch a movie title once you find one you want to watch.

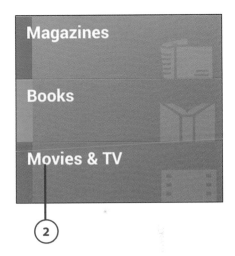

4. Touch to see a trailer of the movie.

5. Touch to expand the synopsis.

6. Scroll down to see all information about the movie including people's reviews and ratings.

7. Touch to share a link to this movie in Google Play to other Android users.

8. Touch to rent the movie in standard definition (not the best quality).

9. Touch to rent the movie in High Definition (HD).

10. Touch to accept and buy or rent the movie.

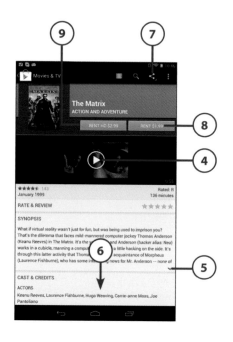

11. Touch to first download the movie to your tablet so that you can watch it when you are not in Wi-Fi coverage.

12. Touch to start watching the movie. This streams the movie to your tablet from the Google cloud.

Movie Download Progress

If you choose to download the movie you rented or purchased because you know you want to watch it when you will be out of Wi-Fi coverage (on a plane for example), you can see the progress of the movie download right on the screen. Wait until it shows "Downloaded" before you move out of Wi-Fi coverage.

Download progress

Buying TV Shows

As with music, when you buy TV shows, they remain in the Google cloud and stream to your tablet when you want to watch them.

1. Touch to launch Google Play.

2. Touch Movies & TV.

3. Touch a TV show title after you find one you want to watch.

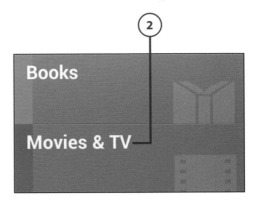

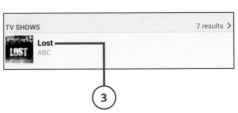

4. Touch to expand the synopsis.

5. Touch to share a link to this TV show in Google Play to other Android users.

6. Touch to change the season if the TV show has multiple seasons.

7. Touch to buy the entire season. When you buy a season that is not yet complete, as new episodes air on TV, you will automatically have access to them on your tablet.

8. Touch to buy just one episode.

9. Touch to buy the Standard Definition (SD) version of the TV show season or episode. SD is lower quality.

10. Touch to buy the High Definition (HD) version of the TV show season or episode. HD is the best quality.

11. Touch to continue.

12. Touch Accept & Buy to complete your purchase.

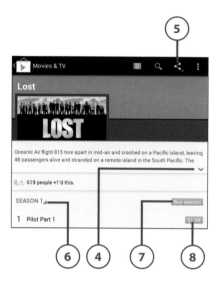

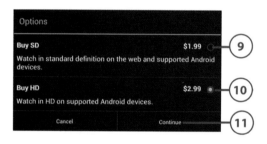

Play Movies & TV App

When you watch movies and TV shows, they are actually playing inside an app called Play Movies & TV. You can launch this app yourself when you want to watch movies and TV shows you have previously purchased or rented.

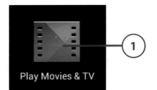

Play Movies & TV

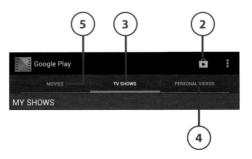

1. Touch to launch Play Movies & TV.

2. Touch to find more movies or TV shows in the Google Play store.

3. Touch to see your TV shows.

4. Touch to see any personal videos you may have loaded.

5. Touch to see your movies.

Movies

After you have movies rented, you can choose to download them to your tablet to view offline, or you can start watching them immediately.

→ A blue push pin indicates that you have downloaded the movie to your tablet and can therefore watch it without a Wi-Fi connection.

→ Touch a grayed-out push pin to download the movie to your tablet so that you can watch it later without a Wi-Fi connection.

Indicates you've downloaded the movie

Touch to download for later viewing

TV Shows

1. Touch a TV show to see episodes you have available.

2. Touch to download the episode to your tablet. Download progress will be indicated by the green background of the push pin.

3. Touch to start watching the episode.

Copying Videos from Your Computer

You can copy videos from your computer onto your Google Nexus Tablet via the USB cable. You start by creating a folder on your tablet to store the videos and then you drag them from your computer to the new folder.

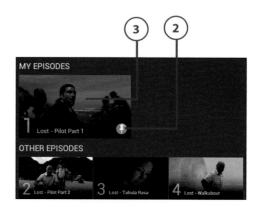

Windows

1. Connect your tablet to your PC using the supplied USB cable. It appears in Windows Explorer.

2. In Explorer, click Nexus 7.

3. Click Internal Storage to expand the list of folders on your Nexus 7.

4. Right-click in the right pane.

5. Click New Folder.

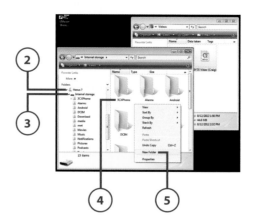

6. Type a name for your new folder. The example folder is My Videos.

7. Click the newly created folder in the left pane.

8. Drag a movie from another folder on your PC to the new folder.

Apple Mac OSX

To copy files from your Mac to your tablet, you must install Android File Transfer. You should have done this already, but if not, please follow the instructions in the Prologue.

1. Connect your tablet to your Mac using the supplied USB cable. Android File Transfer automatically launches.

2. Click File.

3. Click New Folder.

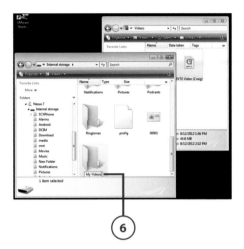

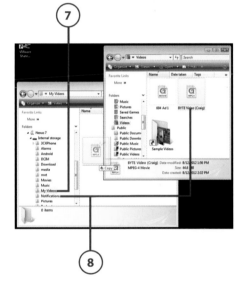

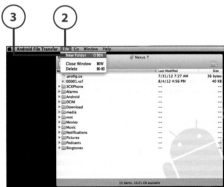

4. Type a name for your new folder
The example folder is My Videos.

5. Drag a movie from another folder
on your Mac to the new folder.

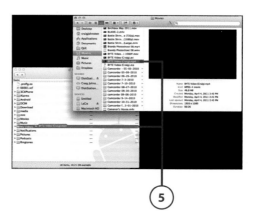

YouTube

Your Google Nexus Tablet comes with a YouTube application that enables
you to find and watch videos, rate them, add them to your favorites, and
share links to YouTube videos. The YouTube application even enables you to
upload new videos.

YouTube Main Screen

1. Touch the YouTube icon to launch the YouTube application.

2. Touch to browse for videos by category, access your YouTube account, and add YouTube channels.

3. Touch to search for a video on YouTube.

4. Touch to change the YouTube app settings.

5. Touch a video to open it.

Browsing for a Video

1. Touch to browse for videos by category.

2. Touch a category.

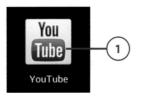

Browse for Videos on a Nexus 10

Since the Nexus 10 has a much bigger screen, the Browse menu is at the top. Touch Browse to see the categories.

3. Touch to search for videos in this category.

4. Type some search criteria.

5. Touch the magnifying glass when you're done typing the search criteria to start the search.

Touch Browse to see the categories

6. Touch to show videos or YouTube Channels.

7. Touch to show only videos that were uploaded to YouTube today, this week, this month, or choose all time to show all videos no matter when they were uploaded.

8. Touch a video to open it.

Playing a Video

While playing a YouTube video, you can rate the video, read video comments, and share the video with someone.

1. Touch to share a link to this video. You can share it on Facebook, Twitter, Google+, or by more traditional ways such as email and text message.

2. Touch to add this video to your favorites, save the video to an existing or new YouTube playlist, or flag the video.

3. Touch to give this video a thumbs up.

4. Touch to give this video a thumbs down.

5. Touch to see videos that are related to this one. YouTube finds videos that are related because of content and key words.

6. Touch to read comments made about this video and write your own.

7. Touch to +1 this video in Google+.

8. Touch to subscribe to the YouTube Channel where this video is found.

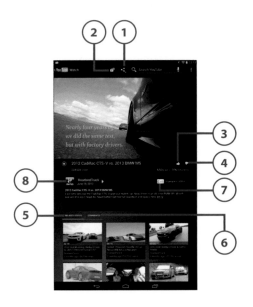

Viewing Videos Full Screen

To view a video at a larger size, simply rotate your Google Nexus Tablet, and the video will be played in landscape mode.

Upload a Video

You can upload one of your personal videos to YouTube.

1. Touch the YouTube logo.

2. Touch your YouTube account.

3. Touch the upload icon.

4. Select a video to upload from videos you have stored in the Gallery app.

5. Touch to enter a title for your video.

6. Touch to enter a description for your video.

7. Touch to choose whether the video is private, public, or unlisted.

8. Touch to add any tags or key words so that your video can be found if people search using the tags you enter.

9. Touch to upload your video.

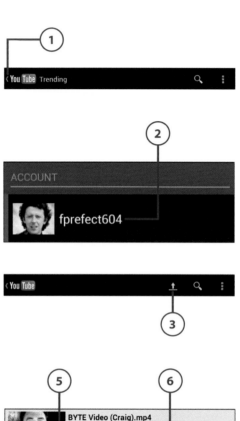

Beaming a YouTube Video

You can send a YouTube video to someone else who has an Android smartphone or tablet with NFC by using Beam. After you Beam the video to the other device, the video loads your friend's YouTube app and automatically starts play.

1. Find a video you want to Beam.

2. Touch your tablet back to back with the other Android device and you should hear a sound. Your screen will zoom out.

3. Touch to Beam the YouTube video to the other device.

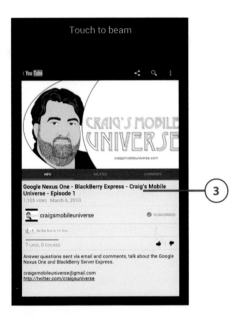

Changing YouTube Settings

If you want to clear your YouTube search history, set the video caption font size, or choose the SafeSearch Filter, you can do this in the YouTube application's settings screen.

1. Touch the Menu button.

2. Touch Settings.

3. Touch General settings.

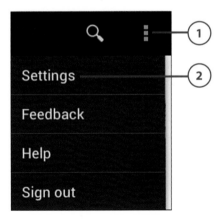

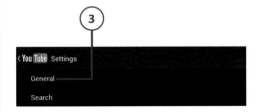

4. Touch to change the video captions font size. You can choose Small, Medium, Large, and Huge.

5. Touch to return to the main settings menu.

6. Touch Search settings.

7. Touch to clear your YouTube search history.

8. Touch to change the SafeSearch filtering options. This allows you to choose whether you want YouTube to filter out certain content. You can select no filtering, moderate filtering, or strict filtering.

9. Touch to return to the main settings menu.

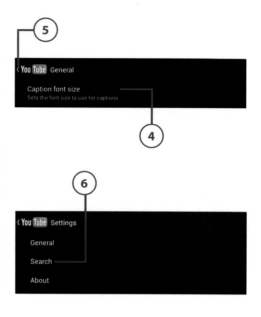

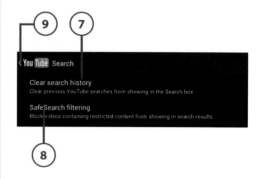

Quickly control
your Bluetooth
and Wi-Fi

This chapter covers your Google Nexus Tablet's connectivity capabilities including Bluetooth, Wi-Fi, Wi-Fi Direct, VPN, and NFC. Topics include the following:

→ Pairing with Bluetooth devices

→ Connecting to Wi-Fi networks

→ Connecting to Virtual Private Networks (VPN)

→ Using Wi-Fi Direct between two Android devices

→ Using Near Field Communications (NFC)

Connecting to Bluetooth, Wi-Fi, and VPNs

Your Google Nexus Tablet can connect to Bluetooth devices such as headsets, computers, and car in-dash systems, as well as to Wi-Fi networks. It has all the connectivity you should expect on a great tablet. Your Google Nexus Tablet can also connect to virtual private networks (VPNs) for access to secure networks and send information between your tablet and another Android device using Wi-Fi Direct.

Connecting to Bluetooth Devices

Bluetooth is a great personal area network (PAN) technology that allows for short distance wireless access to all sorts of devices such as headsets, phones, and computers. The following tasks walk you through how to pair your Google Nexus Tablet to your device and configure options.

Pairing with a New Bluetooth Device

Before you can take advantage of Bluetooth, you need to connect your Google Nexus Tablet with that device, which is called pairing. After you pair your Google Nexus Tablet with a Bluetooth device, they can connect to each other automatically in the future.

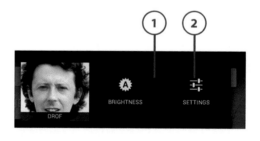

Put the Bluetooth Device into Pairing Mode First

Before you pair a Bluetooth device to your Google Nexus Tablet, you must first put the device into Pairing Mode. If you are pairing with a Bluetooth headset, for example, the process normally involves holding the button on the headset for a certain period of time. Please consult your Bluetooth device's manual to find out how to put that device into Pairing Mode.

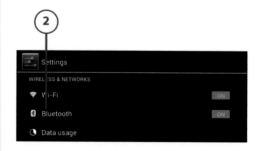

1. Pull down the Quick Settings bar and touch the Full Settings icon.

2. Touch Bluetooth under the Wireless & Networks section.

3. Touch to enable Bluetooth and it automatically begins searching for other Bluetooth devices.

4. Touch the Bluetooth device you want to connect to. This example uses the 390Plantronics headset.

5. If all went well, your Google Nexus Tablet should now be paired with the new Bluetooth device.

Your tablet's Bluetooth name

3

4

Discovered Bluetooth devices

Bluetooth Passkey

If you are pairing with a device that requires a passkey, such as a computer or another smartphone or tablet, the screen shows a passkey. Make sure the passkey is the same on your Google Nexus Tablet and on the device you are pairing with. Touch Pair on your Google Nexus Tablet, and confirm the passkey on the device you are pairing with.

Successfully paired

All Zeros

If you are pairing with an older Bluetooth headset, you might be prompted to enter the passkey. Try using four zeros as the pass-key. It normally works. If the zeros don't work, refer to the headset's manual.

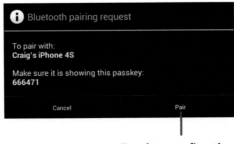

Touch to confirm the passkey and pair

Reverse Pairing

The steps in this section describe how to pair your Google Nexus Tablet with a Bluetooth device that is in Pairing Mode, listening for an incoming pairing command. You can pair Bluetooth another way by putting your Google Nexus in Discovery Mode. To do this, touch the Bluetooth name of your Google Nexus Tablet on the screen (this is normally "Google Nexus Tablet" unless you changed it). Your Google Nexus Tablet goes into pairing mode for two minutes.

Changing Bluetooth Settings

You can change the name your Google Nexus Tablet uses when pairing over Bluetooth, and change the amount of time it remains visible when pairing. Here is how.

1. Touch the Menu button.

2. Touch to rename your Google Nexus Tablet's Bluetooth name.

3. Touch to change how long your Google Nexus Tablet stays visible when pairing.

4. Touch to see any files people have sent you via Bluetooth.

Touch to make your tablet visible for pairing

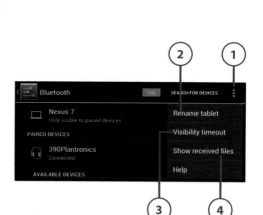

How Long Should I Stay Visible?

When you choose to change your visibility timeout, you can choose 2 minutes, 5 minutes, 1 hour, or never time out. If you think that the person who wants to pair with you may take more than 2 minutes to do it then you'll need to change your visibility timeout. Although you leave the setting on never time out, it is probably not a good idea because every now and then hackers find ways to break into your tablet via Bluetooth using a hacker technique called bluesnarfing. This is very rare. More common is a harmless activity called bluejacking where you can send your vCard to someone's phone if they leave their phone visible.

Changing Bluetooth Device Options

After a Bluetooth device is paired, you can change a few options for some of them. The number of options depends on the Bluetooth device you are connecting to. Some have more features than others.

1. Touch the Settings icon to the right of the Bluetooth device.

2. Touch to rename the Bluetooth device to something more friendly.

3. Touch to disconnect and unpair from the Bluetooth device. If you do this, you won't be able to use the device until you redo the pairing as described in the earlier task.

4. Touch to enable and disable using this device for phone calls. Sometimes Bluetooth devices have more than one profile. You can use this screen to select which ones you want to use.

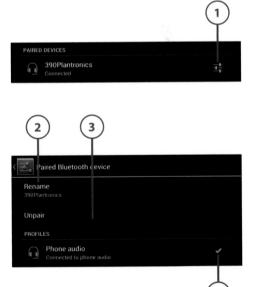

Bluetooth Profiles

Each Bluetooth device can have one or more Bluetooth profiles. Each Bluetooth profile describes certain features of the device. This tells your Google Nexus Tablet what it can do when connected to it. A Bluetooth headset normally only has one profile such as Phone Audio. This tells your Google Nexus Tablet that it can only use the device for phone call audio. Some devices might have this profile but provide other features, such as a Phone Book Access profile, which would enable it to synchronize your Google Nexus Tablet's address book, or Media Audio, which is for playing stereo music via Bluetooth.

Quick Disconnect

To quickly disconnect from a Bluetooth device, touch the device on the Bluetooth Settings screen and then touch OK.

Wi-Fi

Wi-Fi (Wireless Fidelity) networks are wireless networks that run within free radio bands around the world. Your local coffee shop probably has free Wi-Fi, and so do many other places such as airports, train stations, malls, and other public areas. Your Google Nexus Tablet can connect to any Wi-Fi network to provide you access to the Internet.

Connecting to Wi-Fi

The following steps explain how to find and connect to Wi-Fi networks. After you have connected your Google Nexus Tablet to a Wi-Fi network, you are automatically connected to it the next time you are in range of that network.

1.   Pull down the Quick Settings bar and touch the Full Settings icon.

2.   Touch Wi-Fi under the Wireless & Networks section.

3.   Touch to turn Wi-Fi on if the slider is in the off position.

4.   Touch the name of the Wi-Fi network you want to connect to. If the network does not use any security you can skip to Step 7.

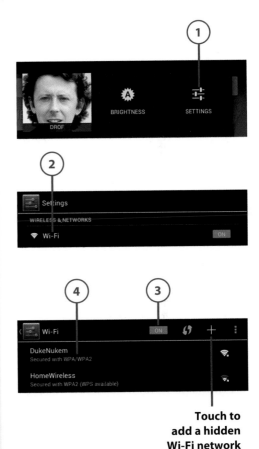

Touch to add a hidden Wi-Fi network

5. Enter the Wi-Fi network password.

6. Touch to connect to the Wi-Fi network.

Adding a Hidden Network

If the network you want to connect to is not listed on the screen, it might be purposely hidden. If it is hidden then it does not broadcast its name, which is also known as its SSID (or Service Set Identifier). You need to touch Add Network, type in the SSID, and choose the type of security that the network uses. You need to get this information from the network administrator before you try connecting.

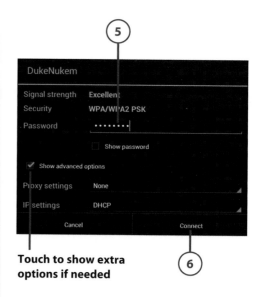

Touch to show extra options if needed

Type network name (SSID)

Choose type of security used (if any)

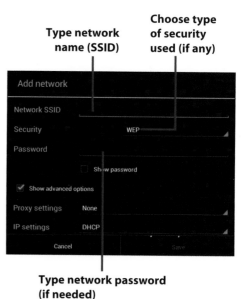

Type network password (if needed)

7. If all goes well you see the Wi-Fi network in the list with the word Connected under it.

Can't Connect to Wi-Fi?

If all does not go well, you might be typing the password or encryption key incorrectly. Verify both with the person who owns the Wi-Fi network. Sometimes there is a lot of radio interference that causes problems. If possible, ask the person who owns the Wi-Fi network to change the channel it operates on and try again.

Connecting to Wi-Fi Protected Setup (WPS) Networks

Many new Wi-Fi routers include a method of connecting called Wi-Fi Protected Setup (WPS). The idea is that on the Wi-Fi router, you press a button to start the WPS connection. On your tablet, you touch the WPS icon and the two devices automatically connect to each other in a secure way. Sometimes a WPS-enabled router uses a method where you swap PINs. Your tablet supports both methods of connecting via WPS.

Indicates Wi-Fi signal strength

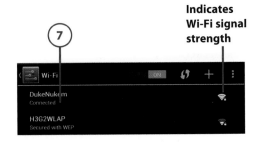

Touch to use the WPS push-button method

Touch to use the WPS PIN method

Wi-Fi Network Options

1. Touch a Wi-Fi network to reveal a pop-up that shows information about your connection to that network.

2. Touch Forget to tell your Google Nexus Tablet to not connect to this network in the future.

3. Touch and hold on a Wi-Fi network to reveal two actions.

4. Touch to forget the Wi-Fi network and no longer connect to it.

5. Touch to change the Wi-Fi network password or encryption key that your Google Nexus Tablet uses to connect to the network.

Advanced Wi-Fi Options

You can configure a few advanced Wi-Fi settings that can actually help preserve the battery life of your Google Nexus Tablet.

1. Touch the Menu button.

2. Touch Advanced.

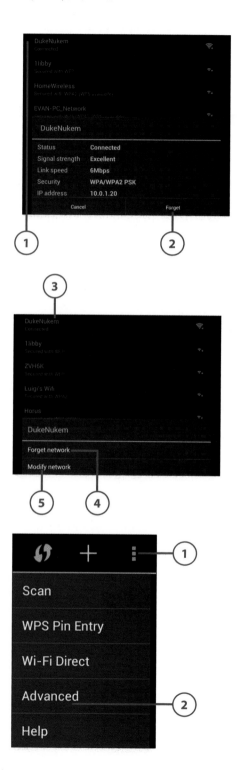

3. Touch to enable or disable the ability for your Google Nexus Tablet to automatically notify you when it detects a new Wi-Fi network.

4. Touch to change the Wi-Fi sleep policy. This enables you to choose if your Google Nexus Tablet should keep its connection to Wi-Fi when the tablet goes to sleep.

5. Use this Wi-Fi MAC address if you need to provide a network administrator with your MAC address in order to be able to use a Wi-Fi network.

6. This shows the IP address that has been assigned to your Google Nexus Tablet when it connected to the Wi-Fi network.

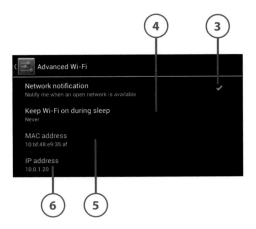

Should You Keep Wi-Fi on During Sleep?

In Step 3 you can choose how your Google Nexus Tablet handles its connection to Wi-Fi when it goes to sleep. Because Wi-Fi is the only way that your tablet can connect to the Internet, you should keep this set to Always, otherwise any real-time updates cannot be delivered to you and your tablet cannot update things such as email. However, battery usage can be affected by always maintaining a Wi-Fi connection, and you might want to set this to Only When Plugged In, which means that if your Google Nexus Tablet is not charging, and it goes to sleep, it turns Wi-Fi off. When the tablet is charging and it goes to sleep, it stays connected to Wi-Fi. If you set this setting to Never, it means that when your Google Nexus Tablet goes to sleep, it turns Wi-Fi off.

>>>Go Further

WHAT ARE IP AND MAC ADDRESSES?

A MAC address is a number burned into your Google Nexus Tablet that identifies its Wi-Fi adapter. This is called the physical layer because it is a physical adapter. An IP address is a secondary way to identify your Google Nexus Tablet. Unlike a MAC address, the IP address can be changed anytime. Modern networks use the IP address when they need to deliver some data to you. Typically when you connect to a network, a device on the network assigns you a new IP address. On home networks, this device is typically your Wi-Fi router.

Some network administrators use a security feature to limit who can connect to their Wi-Fi networks. They set up their networks to only allow connections from Wi-Fi devices with specific MAC addresses. If you are trying to connect to such a network, you have to give the network administrator your MAC address, so he can add it to the allowed list.

Wi-Fi Direct

Wi-Fi Direct is a feature that enables two Android devices running version 4.1 (Jelly Bean) to connect to each other using Wi-Fi for the purpose of exchanging files. Because Wi-Fi is much faster than Bluetooth, if you are sending large files, using Wi-Fi Direct makes sense. Although Wi-Fi Direct is built into Jelly Bean Android devices, such as your Google Nexus Tablet, and you can successfully connect to devices, the actual sending of files between them doesn't work. It appears that Google added the functionality, but never extended it to the apps so they can make use of it.

Setting Up Wi-Fi Direct

In this section we will cover how to use Wi-Fi Direct. As we said before, Wi-Fi Direct doesn't work right now but if this is corrected in the future, these steps should be followed to set it up.

1. Pull down the Quick Settings Bar and touch the Full Settings icon.

2. Touch Wi-Fi under the Wireless & Networks section.

3. Touch the Menu button.

4. Touch Wi-Fi Direct.

5. Touch Rename Device to rename your Google Nexus Tablet from its generic name (in this case Android_18bb) to something more meaningful.

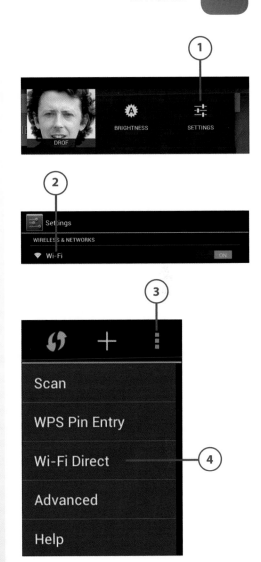

6. Type a new name for your Google Nexus Tablet as it will appear to others using Wi-Fi Direct.

7. Touch OK.

Using Wi-Fi Direct (The Official Way)

These are the steps that must be followed to connect two Android devices running version 4.1 (Jelly Bean) or later via Wi-Fi Direct. After they are connected you should theoretically be able to send files between them but as of the writing of this book, the functionality does not work.

1. Pull down the Quick Settings Bar and touch the Full Settings icon.

2. Touch Wi-Fi under the Wireless & Networks section.

3. Touch the Menu button.

4. Touch Wi-Fi Direct.

5. Ask the other person to enable Wi-Fi Direct on his Android device and its name should appear on your screen.

6. Touch the device to invite it to connect with your Google Nexus Tablet via Wi-Fi Direct. The other person is asked to accept your invitation on his device.

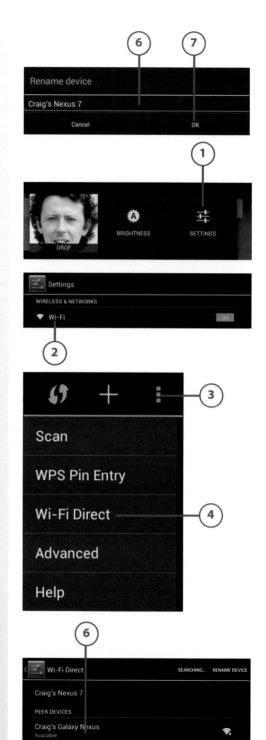

7. The device status shows as "Invited" until the other person accepts your invitation to connect.

After You Are Connected Then What?

After you are connected with another device via Wi-Fi Direct, theoretically you should be able to open a picture, video, or music file and touch the Share icon and see Wi-Fi Direct there. This, however, is not the case, which means that using Wi-Fi Direct doesn't work as of the writing of this book.

Using Wi-Fi Direct (Using WiFi Shoot)

Because the official method of using Wi-Fi Direct doesn't work, you can download an app called WiFi Shoot from Google Play (see Chapter 8, "Working with Android Applications," for more on how to use Google Play). WiFi Shoot isn't perfect, but it should enable you to send files via Wi-Fi Direct. To use WiFi Shoot, you and the person you want to share files with must both install and open WiFi Shoot.

1. Touch the WiFi Shoot icon.

2. Ask the other person to run WiFi Shoot on her Android device. The other person's device should appear on your screen.

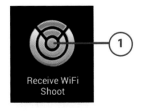

3. Touch the device to invite it to connect with your Google Nexus Tablet via Wi-Fi Direct. The other person is asked to accept your invitation on her device.

4. Touch SHOOT after your two devices connect successfully.

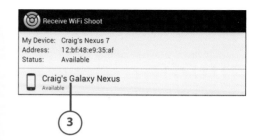

After You Are Connected Then What?

After you are connected with another device via Wi-Fi Direct using WiFi Shoot, you can open a picture, song, video, or any other file on your Google Nexus Tablet and when you touch the Share icon, you should see a new method of sharing called WiFi Shoot. Touch the WiFi Shoot option to send the file to the other device using WiFi Shoot.

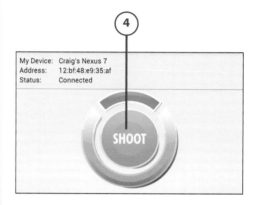

Touch to share the picture

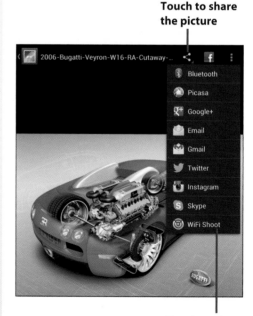

Touch to share via WiFi Shoot

Virtual Private Networks (VPNs)

Your Google Nexus Tablet can connect to virtual private networks (VPNs), which are normally used by companies to provide a secure connection to their inside networks or intranets.

Adding a VPN

Before you add a VPN, you must first have all the information needed to set it up on your Google Nexus Tablet. Speak to your network administrator and get this information ahead of time to save frustration. This information includes the type of VPN protocol used, type of encryption used, and the name of the host to which you are connecting.

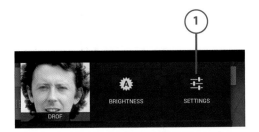

1. Pull down the Quick Settings Bar and touch Full Settings icon.

2. Touch More under the Wireless & Networks section.

3. Touch VPN.

4. Touch OK to set up a lock screen PIN. If you already have a lock screen lock or password, you won't be prompted at this point and you can proceed to Step 8.

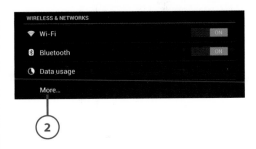

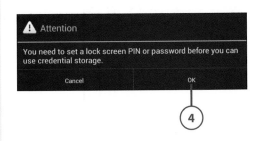

5. Choose either Pattern, PIN, or Password to unlock your Google Nexus Tablet. This example uses a simple PIN.

6. Enter a lock screen PIN.

7. Touch Continue.

8. Touch Add VPN Profile.

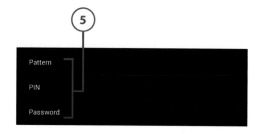

Why Do You Need to Set a PIN?

If you don't already have a lock screen PIN, password, or pattern set up before you create your first VPN network connection, you are prompted to create one. This is a security measure that ensures your Google Nexus Tablet must first be unlocked before anyone can access a stored VPN connection. Because VPN connections are usually used to access company data, this is a good idea.

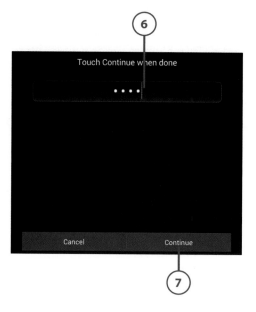

9. Enter a name for your VPN network. You can call it anything like "Work VPN" or the name of the provider like "PublicVPN."

10. Touch to choose the type of security the VPN network uses.

11. Enter the remaining parameters that your network administrator has provided.

12. Touch Save.

Connecting to a VPN

After you have created one or more VPN connections, you can connect to them when the need arises.

1. Pull down the Quick Settings bar and touch the Full Settings icon.

2. Touch More under the Wireless & Networks section.

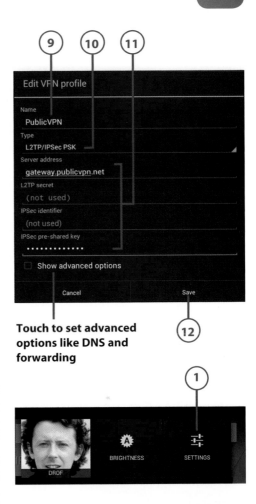

Touch to set advanced options like DNS and forwarding

3. Touch VPN.

4. Touch a pre-configured VPN connection.

5. Enter the VPN username.

6. Enter the VPN password.

7. Touch Connect. After you're con-nected to the VPN, you can use your Google Nexus Tablet's web browser and other applications normally, but you now have access to resources at the other end of the VPN tunnel, such as company web servers or even your company email.

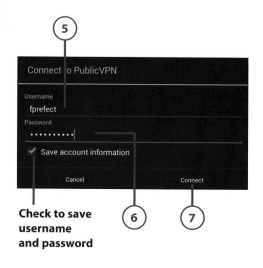

Check to save username and password

Connected to VPN

How Can You Tell If You Are Connected?

After your Google Nexus Tablet successfully connects to a VPN network, you see a key icon in the Notification Bar. This indicates that you are connected. If you pull down the Notification Bar, you can touch the icon to see information about the connection and to disconnect from the VPN.

Touch to view, manage, and disconnect

Edit or Delete a VPN

You can edit an existing VPN or delete it by touching and holding on the name of the VPN. A window pops up with a list of options.

>>>Go Further

ACCESS YOUR VPN QUICKLY

As you can see from the preceding task, it takes three steps to the VPN Settings screen. If you use a VPN connection often and want to cut down on the steps, you can create a shortcut on your Home screen that takes you straight to the VPN Settings screen. To do this, you need to find the Settings Shortcut Widget. Touch and hold it and then drag it to the Home screen where you want it to stay. When you release the widget it shows you a list of settings screens. Touch VPN. Learn more about Home screen widgets in Chapter 9.

Touch and hold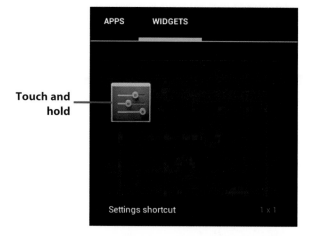

Drag into position and release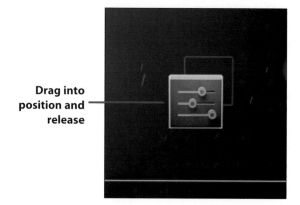

Touch VPN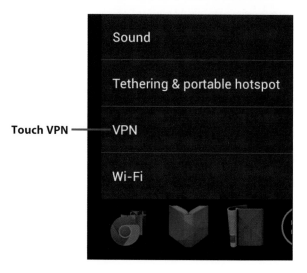

Near Field Communications (NFC)

Your Google Nexus Tablet has the ability to swap data via its Near Field Communications (NFC) radio with other devices that use NFC or read data that is stored on NFC tags. You can also use NFC to pay for items you have purchased using Google Wallet. Here is how to start using NFC.

WHAT IS NFC?

>>>Go Further

NFC stands for Near Field Communications and is a standard that enables devices such as mobile phones or tablets to swap information or simply read information. Think of NFC as a much lower-power version of RFID (Radio Frequency Identification), which has been used for decades in applications like electronic tolls, or etoll payments (when you drive through toll plazas and have the money automatically deducted from your account). The only difference is that with NFC you must bring the two devices within about an inch from each other before they can communicate.

Your Google Nexus Tablet has an NFC radio, which you can use to read NFC tags, swap information between two NFC-enabled devices (such as two NFC-enabled phones or tablets), and send information to another phone or device. As more phones start shipping with NFC built-in, the more this technology will become useful.

Enabling NFC

NFC is enabled by default but just in case you have disabled it, here is how to re-enable it.

1. Pull down the Quick Settings Bar and touch the Full Settings icon.

2. Touch More.

3. Touch to enable NFC data exchange.

Touch to
open email

Touch to
open Gmail
email

In this chapter, you find out about your Google Nexus Tablet's email applications for Gmail and other email accounts such as POP3, IMAP, and even your corporate email. Topics include the following:

→ Sending and receiving email
→ Working with attachments
→ Working with Gmail labels
→ Changing settings

Email

Your Google Nexus Tablet has two email programs: the Gmail app, which only works with Gmail, and the Email app that works with POP3, IMAP, and corporate email systems such as Microsoft Exchange and Lotus Notes.

Gmail

When you first set up your Google Nexus Tablet, you set up a Gmail account. The Gmail application enables you to have multiple Gmail accounts, which is useful if you have a business account and a personal account.

Adding a Google Account

When you first set up your Google Nexus Tablet, you added your first Google (Gmail) account. The following steps describe how to add a second account.

1. Touch to open the Gmail app.

2. Touch the Menu button.

3. Touch Settings.

4. Touch Add Account.

5. Touch Existing to use an existing Google account.

What If I Don't Have a Second Google Account?

If you don't already have a second Google account, but want to set one up, in Step 5, touch New. Your Google Nexus Tablet walks you through the steps of setting up a new Google account.

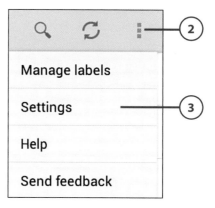

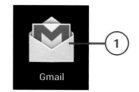

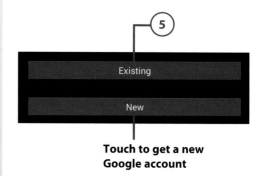

Touch to get a new
Google account

6. Enter your existing Google account name. This is your Gmail address.

7. Enter your existing Google password.

8. Touch to sign in to your Google account.

9. Select what components of your Google account you want to synchronize with your Galaxy Nexus and then touch the right arrow at the bottom of the screen to finish the Google account setup.

Why Multiple Google Accounts?

You are probably wondering why you would want multiple Google accounts. Isn't one good enough? Actually it is not that uncommon to have multiple Google accounts. It can be a way to compartmentalize your life between work and play. You might run a small business using the one account, but email only friends with another. Your Google Nexus Tablet supports multiple accounts but still enables you to interact with them in one place.

Navigating the Gmail App

Let's take a quick look at the Gmail app and find out how to navigate the main screen.

1. Touch the Gmail icon to launch the app.

2. Touch to switch between Gmail accounts (if you use more than one).

3. Indicates how many unread messages you have in the selected label.

4. Touch the Menu button to see the menu.

5. Touch to manage your labels including changing which labels synchronize to your Google Nexus Tablet.

6. Touch to compose a new email.

7. Touch to search the current label for an email.

8. Touch to manually refresh the current view.

9. Touch a label to switch to it.

10. Touch the star to add the email to the Starred label.

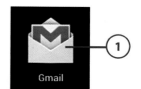

Indicates that Google has marked the email as important

Stars and Labels

In Gmail, you use stars and labels to help organize your email. In most email clients you can create folders in your mailbox to help you organize your emails. For example you might create a folder called "emails from the boss" and move any emails you receive from your boss to that folder. Gmail doesn't use the term *folders*; it uses the term *labels* instead. You can create labels in Gmail and choose an email to label. When you do this, it actually moves it to a folder with that label, but to you, the email has a label distinguishing it from other emails. Any email that you mark with a star is actually just getting a label called "starred." But when viewing your Gmail, you see the yellow star next to an email. People normally add a star to an email as a reminder of something important.

Composing Gmail Email

1. Touch the compose icon.

2. Touch to change the Gmail account from which the message is being sent (if you have multiple Gmail accounts).

3. Type names in the To field. If the name matches someone in your Contacts, a list of choices is displayed and you can touch a name to select it.

4. Touch to add Carbon Copy (CC) or Blind Carbon Copy (BCC) recipients.

5. Touch the paperclip icon to add one or more picture attachments.

6. Type a subject for your email.

7. Type the body of the email.

8. Touch to send the email.

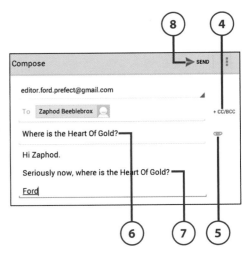

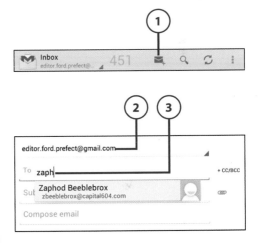

Add Picture Attachments

Before sending an email you can add one or more picture attachments. The Gmail app does not allow you to attach other kinds of attachments—just pictures that are in the Gallery app. Here is how to add picture attachments.

1. Touch the paperclip icon.

2. Navigate the Gallery App and touch the picture you want to attach.

3. Touch Send.

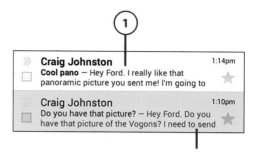

Touch to remove the attachment

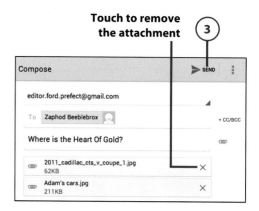

Reading Gmail Email

1. Touch an email to open it.

Gray shading indicates an email has already been read

2. Touch to add additional labels to the email.

3. Touch to reply to the sender of the email. This does not reply to anyone in the CC field.

4. Touch to reply to the sender of the email and any recipients in the To and CC fields.

5. Touch to forward the email to someone.

6. Touch to expand the email header to see all recipients and all other email header information.

7. Touch to "star" the message, or move it to the "starred" label.

8. Indicates whether the sender of the email is online using Google Talk (GTalk) if that person is in your GTalk buddy list.

9. Touch to move the email to the Gmail Archive folder.

10. Touch to move the email to the Trash folder.

11. Touch to mark the email as unread and return to the email list view.

12. Touch the Menu button to take more actions on the message.

13. Touch to report the email as spam.

14. Touch to mute the email conversation. Once muted, you no longer see emails in the conversation.

15. Touch to mark the message as not important or important.

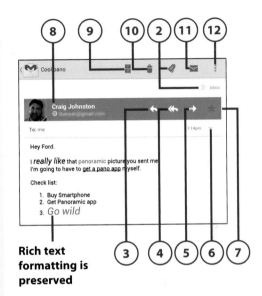

Rich text formatting is preserved

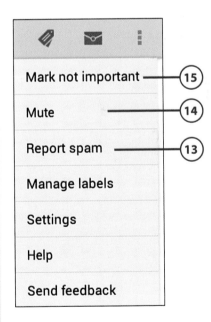

Rich Text Formatting

Rich Text Formatting (RTF) is a message formatted with anything that is not plain text. RTF includes bulleted lists, different fonts, font colors, font sizes, and styles such as bold, italic, and underline. Although you cannot type an email on your tablet with the standard keyboard using RTF, if you are sent an email with RTF in it, your tablet preserves the formatting and displays it correctly.

What Are Conversations?

Conversations are Gmail's version of email threads. When you look at the main view of the Gmail app, you are seeing a list of email conversations. The conversation might have only one email in it, but to Gmail that's a conversation. As you and others reply to that original email, Gmail groups those emails in a thread, or conversation.

What Is Important?

Gmail tries to automatically figure out which of the emails you receive are important. As it learns it might get it wrong. If an email is marked as important but it is not important, you can change the status to not important manually as described in Step 15. Important emails have a yellow arrow whereas emails that are not important have a clear arrow. All emails marked as Important are also given the Priority Inbox label.

What Happens to Your Spam?

When you mark an email in Gmail as spam, two things happen. Firstly it gets a label called Spam. Secondly a copy of that email is sent to Gmail's spam servers so they are now aware of a possible new spam email that is circulating around the Internet. Based on what the servers see for all Gmail users, they block that spam email from reaching other Gmail users. So the bottom line is that you should always mark spam emails because it helps all of us.

Gmail Settings

You can customize the way Gmail accounts work on your Google Nexus Tablet including changing the email signature and choosing which labels synchronize from the Google servers to your tablet.

1. Touch the Menu button.

2. Touch Settings.

3. Touch General Settings.

Email Signature

An email signature is a bit of text that is automatically added to the bottom of any email you send from your Google Nexus Tablet. It is added when you compose a new email, reply to an email, or forward an email. A typical use for a signature is to automatically add your name and maybe some contact information at the end of your emails. Email signatures are sometimes referred to as email footers.

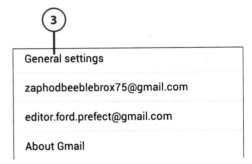

4. Touch to enable or disable confirmation before deleting a message or entire conversation.

5. Touch to enable or disable confirmation before archiving a message or entire conversation.

6. Touch to enable or disable confirmation before sending an email.

7. Touch Auto-advance to select which screen your Google Nexus Tablet must show after you delete or archive and email. Your choices are Newer Conversation, Older Conversation, and Conversation List.

8. Touch to select the size of the text used when reading emails. Your choices range from Tiny to Huge.

9. Touch to clear the Gmail search history.

10. Touch to restore the setting for whether to automatically load pictures when reading email. By default this is set to off.

11. Touch to return to the main Settings screen.

12. Touch one of your Gmail accounts to change settings specific to that account.

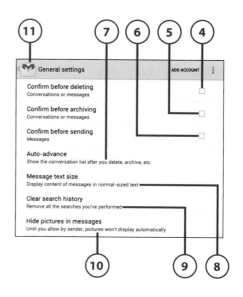

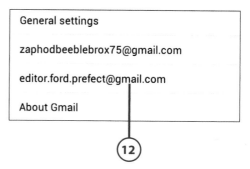

13. Touch to enable or disable showing your Priority Inbox instead of your regular Inbox when opening the Gmail app.

14. Touch to enable or disable notifications when new email arrives for this Gmail account.

15. Touch to select how to get notified when new email arrives for this account. You can choose.

16. Touch to enter a signature that will appear at the end of all emails composed using this account.

17. Touch to change how this account is synchronized, what is synchronized, or remove it entirely.

18. Touch to select how many days of mail to synchronize with your Google Nexus Tablet.

19. Touch to manage labels. See more about managing labels in the next section.

20. Touch to enable or disable automatically downloading attachments to recently received emails while connected to a Wi-Fi network.

21. Touch to return to the main Settings screen.

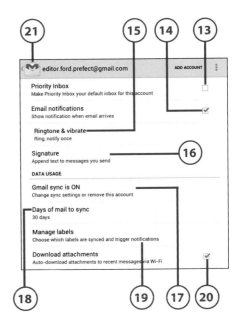

What Is the Priority Inbox?

Google introduced the Priority Inbox as a way to automatically figure out which emails are important to you and place them in a folder called Priority Inbox. It does this by analyzing which emails you open and reply to. If it makes a mistake, you can mark a message as less important or more important. Over time, Google's handle on which emails are important to you gets more accurate. Because the Priority Inbox probably has the most important emails, you might want to open it first and then go to the regular Inbox later to handle less important emails. Read more about the Priority Inbox at http://mail.google.com/mail/help/priority-inbox.html.

Managing Gmail Label Syncing and Alerting

Gmail Labels are Google's name for email folders. You can manage how each of them synchronize to your tablet and alert you.

1. Touch the Menu button.

2. Touch Manage Labels.

3. Touch a label to manage it.

4. Touch to enable synchronization of this label to your Google Nexus Tablet and designate whether to synchronize 30 days of email or all email. When synchronization is enabled, the rest of the settings on this screen become available.

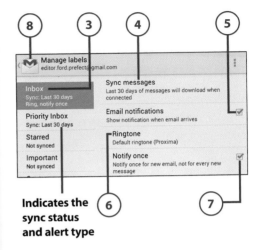

5. Touch to enable or disable being notified when new email arrives in this label.

6. Touch to select the ringtone that plays when you are notified of new email in this label.

7. Touch to enable or disable notifying you once when multiple emails arrive in this label, as opposed to notifying for each one.

8. Touch to return to the main Gmail screen.

Email Application

The Email application supports all email accounts with the exception of Gmail. This includes any corporate email accounts that use Microsoft Exchange, or corporate email systems such as Lotus Domino/Notes that have an ActiveSync gateway. In addition to corporate emails accounts, the Email application also supports POP3 and IMAP accounts. These are typically hosted by your Internet service provider (ISP) as well as by companies such as Yahoo! or Hotmail.

Adding a Corporate Email Account

Chapter 1, "People (Contacts)," covers adding a corporate email account in the "Adding Accounts" section. Please flip back to Chapter 1 if you want to add a corporate account.

Adding a New POP3 or IMAP Account

You can skip to the next section if you don't want to add a POP or IMAP email account.

1. Touch the Settings icon.

2. Touch Add Account under the Accounts section.

3. Touch Email.

4. Enter your email address.

5. Enter your password.

6. Touch Next.

Why Manual Setup?

Your Google Nexus Tablet tries to figure out the settings to set up your email account. This works most of the time when you are using common email providers such as Yahoo! or Hotmail. It also works with large ISPs such as Comcast, Road Runner, Optimum Online, and so on. It might not work for smaller ISPs, or in smaller countries, or if you have created your own website and set up your own email. In these cases, you need to set up your email manually.

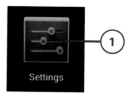

Settings

+ Add account

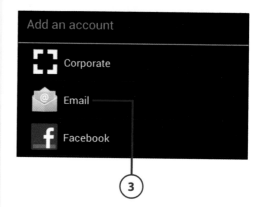

Add an account

Corporate

Email

Facebook

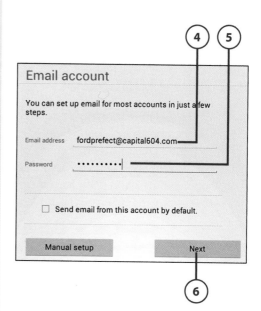

Email account

You can set up email for most accounts in just a few steps.

Email address   fordprefect@capital604.com

Password   ●●●●●●●●●●

☐ Send email from this account by default.

Manual setup   Next

7. Touch POP3 or IMAP. IMAP has more intelligence to it, so select that option where possible.

8. Ensure that the information on this screen is accurate.

9. Touch Next.

Where Can I Find This Information?

If you need to manually set up your email account, you must have a few pieces of information. Always check your ISP's, or email service provider's, website and look for instructions on how to set up your email on a computer or smartphone. This is normally under the support section of the website.

Username and Password

On the Incoming Server and Outgoing Server screens, your username and password should already be filled out because you typed them in earlier. If not, enter them.

10. Ensure that the information on this screen is accurate.

11. Touch Next.

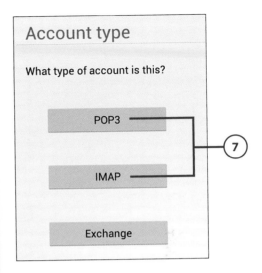

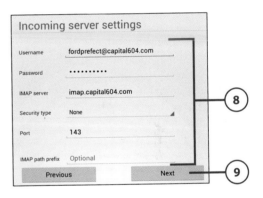

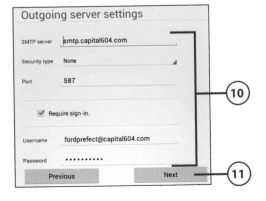

12. Touch to change the frequency in which email from this account synchronizes to your Google Nexus Tablet.

13. Touch to check the box if you want email to be sent from this account by default.

14. Touch to check the box if you want to be notified when new email arrives into this account.

15. Touch to check the box if you want email to synchronize between this account and your Google Nexus Tablet.

16. Touch to check the box if you want email to be automatically downloaded when you are connected to a Wi-Fi network.

17. Touch Next.

18. Enter a friendly name for this account, such as "Work Email".

19. Enter your full name or the name you want to be displayed when people receive emails sent from this account.

20. Touch Next to save the settings for this account and return to the Add Accounts screen.

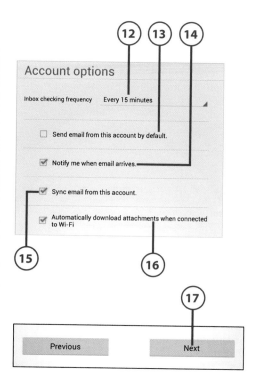

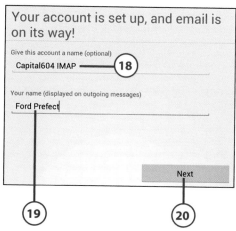

Be Secure If You Can

If your mail provider supports email security such as SSL or TLS, you should strongly consider using it. If you don't, emails you send and receive go over the Internet in plain readable text. Using SSL or TLS encrypts the emails as they travel across the Internet so nobody can read them. Set this under the Advanced settings for the Incoming and Outgoing Servers.

Working with the Email App

Everything you do in the Email application is the same for every email account (if you have more than one account). The Email app enables you to either work with email accounts separately or in a combined view.

Navigating the Email Application

Before you learn how to compose or read emails, you should become familiar with the Email application.

1. Touch to launch the Email app.

2. Touch to switch between email accounts or select the Combined view, which shows all emails from all accounts.

3. Indicates the number of unread emails in the current folder.

4. Touch the star to mark an email as flagged.

5. Each color represents a specific email account.

6. Check boxes next to emails to select more than one. Then you can take actions against multiple emails at once, such as Mark as Read, Flag, Delete, or Move to a new folder.

7. Touch the Menu button to change the Email app settings.

8. Touch to switch between mail accounts when in the Combined view.

9. Touch to compose a new email.

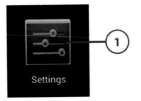

Settings

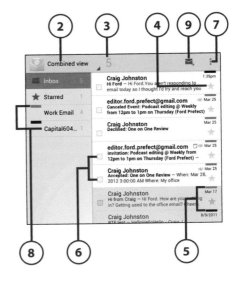

Composing Email

1. Touch to compose a new email.

2. Enter one or more recipients. As you type, your Google Nexus Tablet tries to guess who you want to address the message to. If you see the correct name, touch it to select it. This includes names stored on your Google Nexus Tablet and in your company's corporate address book.

Indicates the mail account being used

3. Touch to add Carbon Copy (CC) and Blind Carbon Copy (BCC) recipients.

4. Touch to attach one or more pictures.

5. Enter a subject.

6. Enter the body of the message.

7. Touch to send the message.

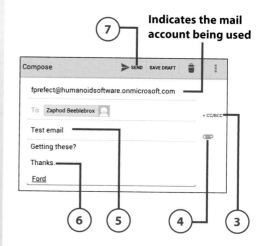

Indicates the mail account being used

It's Not All Good

Cannot Change Account Being Used

While composing an email you cannot change the account that you are using to send the email. It is visually indicated on the screen but you cannot modify it. The default account is always used. See the "Email App Settings" section later in the chapter to find out how to change the default account.

Add Attachments

Before you send your message you might want to add one or more attachments. Unfortunately you can only attach pictures from the Gallery.

1. Touch the paper clip icon.

2. Select a picture to attach.

3. Touch to send the email.

Can You Attach Other Files?

Although the Gmail app and the Email app actually support any attachment type, the apps themselves only let you attach pictures. To send other attachment types via Gmail or Email, you must install a file manager app such as ASTRO. After you have a file manager installed, when you touch the paper clip icon to attach a file you can choose between the default action of opening the Gallery app or the using the file manager (in this case ASTRO).

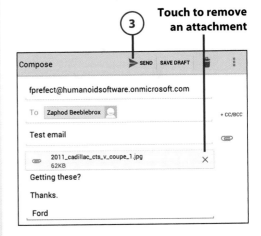

Touch to remove an attachment

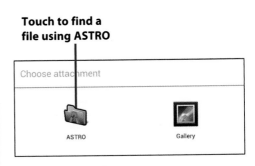

Touch to find a file using ASTRO

Reading Email

Reading messages in the Email application is the same regardless of which account the email has come to.

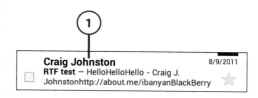

1. Touch an email to read it.

2. Touch to reply to the sender of the email. This does not reply to anyone in the CC field.

3. Touch to reply to the sender of the email and any recipients in the To and CC fields.

4. Touch to forward the email to someone.

5. Touch to expand the email header to see all recipients and all other email header information.

6. Touch the star icon to mark the message as flagged for follow-up.

7. Indicates whether the sender of the email is online using Google Talk (GTalk) if that person is in your GTalk buddy list.

8. Touch to delete the email.

9. Touch to move the email to a folder, including moving it to the Spam folder.

10. Touch to mark the email as unread and return to the email list view.

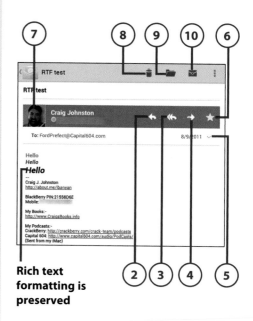

Rich text formatting is preserved

Rich Text Formatting

Rich Text Formatting (RTF) is a message formatted with anything that is not plain text. RTF includes bulleted lists, different fonts, font colors, font sizes, and styles such as bold, italic, and underline. Although you cannot type an email on your tablet with the standard keyboard using RTF, if you are sent an email with RTF in it, your tablet preserves the formatting and displays it correctly.

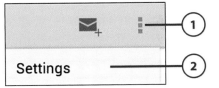

Email App Settings

1. Touch the Menu button.

2. Touch Settings.

3. Touch General.

4. Touch to change how auto-advance works. You can choose to either advance to a newer message, older message, or back to the message list.

5. Touch to change the size of the font used when reading messages. Your choices range from Tiny to Huge.

6. Touch to restore the default for Ask to Show Pictures. By default pictures do not load when you open messages, but you might have changed this for a message you received. This sets it back to the default setting of not showing pictures.

7. Touch to go back to the main Settings screen.

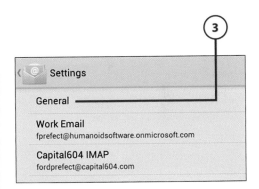

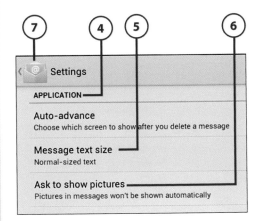

POP/IMAP Account Settings

1. Touch a POP or IMAP account.

2. Touch to change the account name.

3. Touch to change the name that recipients see when you send them email from this account.

4. Touch to add an email signature or edit the one you already have.

5. Touch to add or edit Quick Responses.

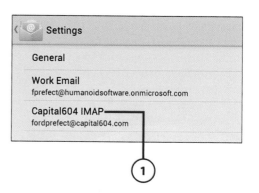

Quick Responses

Quick Responses are words, phrases, sentences, or paragraphs of text that you create ahead of time and save as Quick Responses. While you are composing an email you can choose to insert one or more of your Quick Responses. The idea is that it saves on typing the same things over and over.

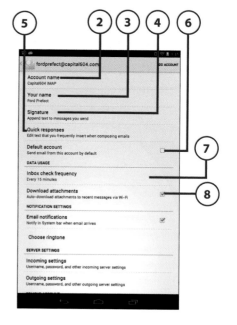

6. Touch to check the box if you want this account to be used as the default account when composing email.

7. Touch to change the frequency at which the Email app checks this account's Inbox for new email.

8. Touch to check the box if you want attachments to automatically download while you are connected to a Wi-Fi network.

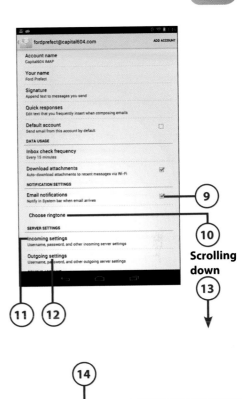

9. Touch to check the box if you want notifications when new email arrives in this accounts Inbox.

10. Touch to choose the ringtone that plays when your are notified of new email for this account.

11. Touch to change the incoming mail server settings for this account. This includes your account username and password if this has changed.

12. Touch to change the outgoing mail server settings for this account. This includes your account username and password if this has changed.

13. Scroll down for more settings.

14. Touch to remove this account.

15. Touch to return to the Settings main screen.

Corporate Account Settings

You are able to change your email signature. You can also control what components to synchronize and how often they synchronize.

1. Touch a corporate account.

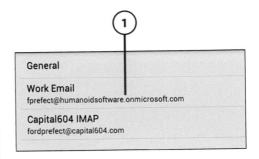

2. Touch to change the account name.

3. Touch to change the name that recipients see when you send them email from this account.

4. Touch to change an email signature or edit the one you already have.

5. Touch to add or edit Quick Responses.

6. Touch to check the box if you want this account to be used as the default account when composing email.

7. Touch to change the frequency at which the Email app checks this account's Inbox for new email. You can also choose Push, which means that emails are pushed to your Google Nexus Tablet in real time as they arrive in your corporate Inbox.

8. Touch to choose how many days of email to synchronize to your Google Nexus Tablet. You can choose between One Day and One Month, or choose All to synchronize every email ever received.

9. Touch to check the box if you want email to synchronize to your Google Nexus Tablet from this corporate account.

10. Touch to check the box if you want contacts to synchronize to your Google Nexus Tablet from this corporate account.

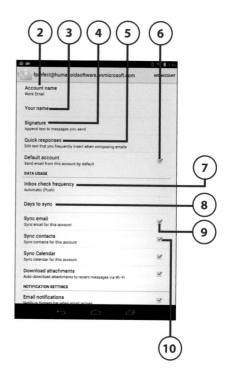

11. Touch to check the box if you want the calendar to synchronize to your Google Nexus Tablet from this corporate account.

12. Touch to check the box if you want attachments to automatically download while you are connected to a Wi-Fi network.

13. Scroll down for more settings.

14. Touch to check the box if you want notifications when new email arrives in this account's Inbox.

15. Touch to choose the ringtone that plays when your are notified of new email for this account.

16. Touch to change the incoming mail server settings for this account. This includes your account username and password if this has changed.

17. Touch to remove this account.

18. Touch to return to the Settings main screen.

Scrolling down

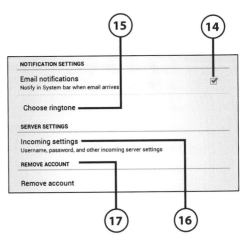

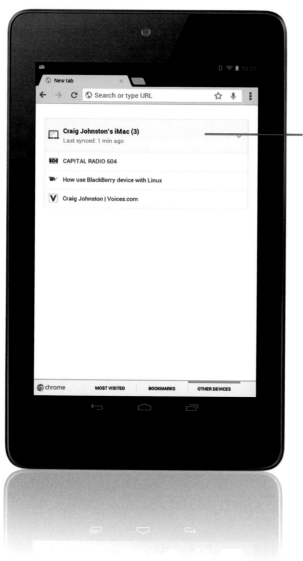

Access bookmarks
on your computer

In this chapter, you discover how to browse the World Wide Web using the browser capabilities of your Google Nexus Tablet. Topics include the following:

→ Bookmarking websites

→ Sharing websites with your friends

→ Keeping track of sites you have visited

→ Using GPS and browsing together

→ Browsing Incognito

Browsing the Web with Chrome

Your Google Nexus Tablet has a fully featured web browser called Chrome. In fact, the experience of using the Google Nexus Tablet's browser is similar to using a desktop browser, just with a smaller screen. You can bookmark sites, hold your Google Nexus Tablet sideways to fit more onto the screen, and even share your GPS location with sites.

Navigating with Chrome

Let's dive right in and cover how to run the Chrome web browser and use all of its features. You can customize your Google Nexus Tablet's browser, share your GPS location, bookmark sites, maintain your browsing history, and even access bookmarks stored on your computer.

Getting Started with Chrome

1. Touch the Chrome icon in the Google folder on the Home screen.

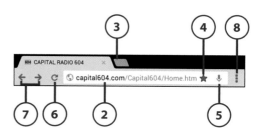

Chrome

2. Touch to type in a new web address. Some websites move the web page up to hide the address field. When this happens, you can drag the web page down to reveal the address bar again.

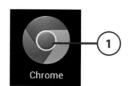

3. Touch to open a new browser tab from which you can go to a new website.

4. Touch to bookmark the website. If the site is already bookmarked you can edit the bookmark.

5. Touch to search the Internet by speaking or to say the name of a website you want to go to.

6. Touch to manually refresh the website.

7. Touch to go to the previous or next page on the current website, or to go to a previous or next website.

8. Touch the Menu button see more options, like finding a word on the web page.

Web Page and Chrome Options

While a web page is open you have a number of options such as finding text on a web page and forcing Chrome to load the desktop version of a web site.

1. Touch the Menu button.

2. Touch to open a new browser tab.

3. Touch to open a new Incognito browser tab.

4. Touch to open the Chrome bookmarks screen.

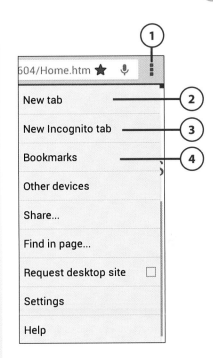

Browse in Secret (Going Incognito)

If you want to visit a website in secret, you can. Visiting a website in secret means that the site you visit does not appear in your browser history or search history and does not otherwise leave a trace of itself on your Google Nexus Tablet. To do this you must create a new Incognito browser tab. Inside that browser tab, all sites you visit are in secret. To create a new Incognito browser tab, while in the browser tab screen, touch the Menu button and touch New Incognito Tab. When you have Incognito tabs open, a new icon appears on the top right that enables you to switch between regular browser tabs and Incognito tabs.

Touch to switch between regular and Incognito tabs

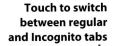

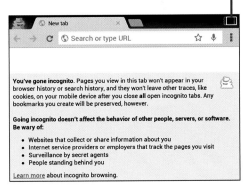

5. Touch to see open browser tabs in Chrome on your desktop computer.

6. Touch to share the current web page's address via Facebook, Twitter, Skype, Bluetooth, or email.

7. Touch to find a word on the current web page.

8. Touch to request the desktop version of the current website if you are seeing a mobile version. When you check the box, Chrome refreshes the page with the desktop version.

9. Touch to change the Chrome web browser settings.

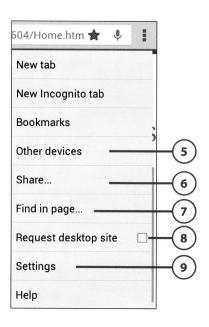

How Can I See My Desktop Computer's Browser Tabs?

To see your desktop computer's Chrome browser tabs, make sure you install Chrome on your desktop computer and use it as your default web browser. Then not only are your bookmarks kept in sync between your tablet and desktop, but any browser tabs you have open in Chrome on your desktop computer (called browser windows on the desktop version of Chrome), are visible and can be opened as described in Step 5. Even if you close Chrome and shut down your computer, you still see the last tabs that were open.

Browser tabs (windows) on your desktop

Browser tabs on your tablet

Chrome Browser Tricks

Your Google Nexus Tablet has some unique tricks to help you browse regular websites on a small screen.

1. Rotate your Google Nexus Tablet on its side, which puts the tablet into what's called *landscape orientation*. Your Google Nexus Tablet automatically switches the screen to landscape mode.

Portrait

Landscape

Zoomed out

2. Double-tap the screen to zoom in and out.

3. If menu choices on a web page are too small, when you touch a menu item, the Chrome browser shows you a zoomed in portion of the menu to enable you to more easily touch your menu item.

Pinch to Zoom

An alternative way to zoom, which allows you to actually zoom in much further, is to place your thumb and forefinger on the screen and spread them apart to zoom in and then move them back together to zoom out.

Zoomed in

Zoomed with pinch to zoom

Landscape Is Not Working for Me

If you rotate your tablet onto its side and the web page doesn't rotate into landscape mode, you might have the rotate lock enabled. Pull down the Quick Settings Bar and make sure the rotation lock is not enabled. If it is, touch it to disable.

Zoomed into menu choices

Rotate lock enabled

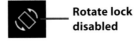
Rotate lock disabled

Managing Bookmarks and History

Your Google Nexus Tablet enables you to bookmark your favorite websites, but it also keeps track of where you have browsed and can show you your browsing history broken up by days, weeks, and months. The history also enables you to read web pages offline.

1. Touch the Menu button.

2. Touch Bookmarks.

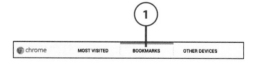

Bookmarks

1. Touch Bookmarks.

2. Touch to see bookmarks and bookmark folders that have been synchronized from your desktop version of Chrome.

3. Touch to see bookmarks in the Other Bookmarks folder on your desktop computer.

4. Touch to see bookmarks that have been saved only on your tablet.

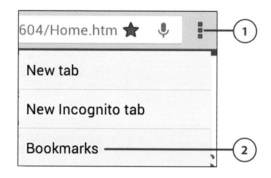

Working With Bookmarks

1. Touch a bookmark to open it in the current tab.

2. Touch and hold a bookmark to see more options.

3. Touch to open the bookmark in a new browser tab.

4. Touch to open the bookmark in an Incognito tab (secretive browsing).

5. Touch to edit the bookmark.

6. Touch to delete the bookmark.

7. Touch to add the bookmark to the Home screen on your tablet.

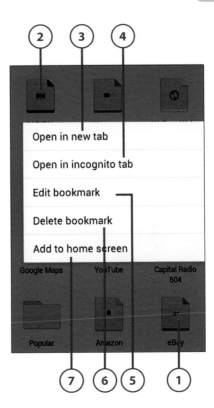

Adding a Bookmark

While you are viewing a web page, you can add it to your list of bookmarks.

1. Touch the star icon in the address bar.

2. Change the bookmark name if you want to. It defaults to the web page's title.

3. Edit the web page link if you want to or leave it as it (normally best).

4. Select the account to save the bookmark under. You can choose to save it in Mobile Bookmarks (only on your tablet) or in one of the bookmark folders that you have synchronized from your desktop computer.

5. Touch to save the bookmark.

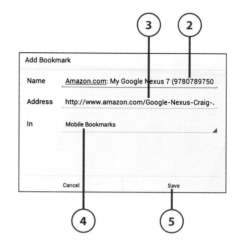

Where to Save Bookmarks

When you save bookmarks, you can choose to save them locally or to one of your desktop bookmark folders. If you choose to save a bookmark locally, it is only saved to your Google Nexus Tablet. The bookmark is not synchronized to the Google cloud or made available anywhere other than on your tablet. If you choose to save the bookmark to one of your desktop bookmark folders, that bookmark is stored in the Google cloud and is then available to you on any device where you use that same Google account. This includes when you log in to your Google account on your desktop version of the Chrome browser on your computer and any Android smartphone or tablet that you purchase and use in the future.

Browsing History

As of the writing of this book, it appears that Google has forgotten to include an easy way of seeing and managing your browser history. You have to use a little trick to be able to see and manage the stored browser history.

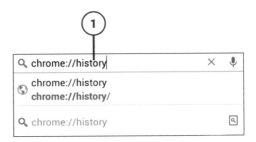

1. Type chrome://history in the address bar.

2. Touch the Go key on the onscreen keyboard.

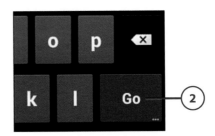

3. Touch to clear all browsing history (this feature didn't work at the time the book went to press).

4. Touch to select the browser history entry and see more options.

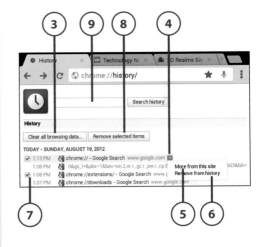

5. Touch to see more history entries related to this one.

6. Touch to remove just this one entry.

7. Touch to select or deselect an entry.

8. Touch to remove entries that have been selected.

9. Touch to search for an entry.

Working with Multiple Open Tabs

As you have seen, you can open multiple browser tabs each with their own websites loaded. As you open more and more tabs, Chrome collapses some of them on the screen to maximize space. To see the collapsed tabs, swipe from left to right or right to left over the tabs and they scroll.

**Tabs collapsed to
maximize space**

**Swipe to reveal
collapsed tabs**

Gray Web Page

Sometimes when you have a lot of tabs open, Chrome conserves memory by freezing pages in tabs that you haven't opened in a while. If you switch to that tab you see your web page but it's in all gray. Chrome refreshes the page, it goes back to normal.

Gray web page

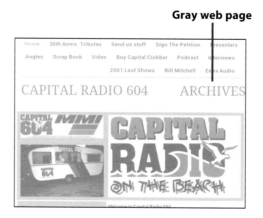

Customizing Browser Settings

Your Google Nexus Tablet's Chrome browser is customizable. Here are the different settings you can adjust.

Adjusting Chrome Settings

1. Touch the Menu button.

2. Touch Settings.

3. Touch your Google account.

4. Touch to enable or disable synchronization, and choose what to synchronize.

5. Touch to enable or disable sending web pages on your desktop version of Chrome to your tablet.

6. Touch to enable or disable automatically signing you in when you browse to a Google website.

7. Touch to return to the main Settings screen.

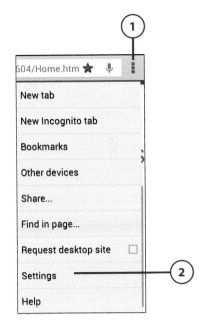

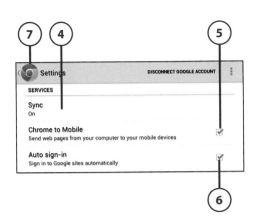

8. Touch to choose the search engine to use. You can choose Google, Yahoo!, or Bing.

9. Touch to enable or disable the Autofill forms feature and create profiles that contain your information and credit card information for Chrome to use in those forms.

10. Touch to enable or disable the ability for Chrome to save your website passwords. This setting also enables you to view and remove any passwords already stored.

11. Touch to see the Privacy settings. Read more about Chrome privacy settings and what information is sent for each setting here at http://support.google.com /chromeos/bin/answer.py?hl=en& answer=1047334&topic=2586066 &ctx=topic.

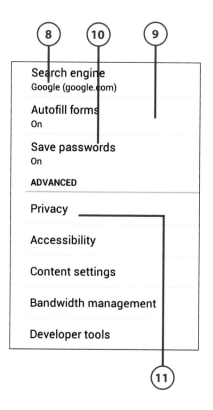

12. Touch to enable or disable Chrome suggesting alternatives when you mistype a website address. If enabled, Chrome sends Google what you have typed in the address bar.

13. Touch to enable or disable Chrome making suggestions as you type in the address bar. If enabled, Chrome sends Google what you have typed in the address bar.

14. Touch to enable or disable the feature where Chrome preloads the IP address of every link on a web page to speed up browsing. If enabled, Chrome sends Google the name of the website you are visiting.

15. Touch to enable or disable sending crash reports, and how they are sent. If enabled, Chrome might send personal information to Google.

16. Touch to return to the main Settings screen.

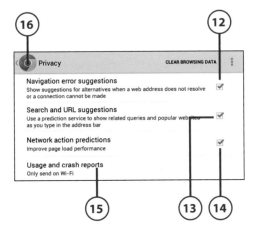

Where Does My Personal Information Go?

In Steps 12–15 you see options to allow Chrome to send your personal information to Google. In each case the information is either used to make your web browsing experience quicker and easier or to help Google figure out why the Chrome browser is crashing. For example, in Step 15 you can allow Chrome to send information about what you were busy doing when the Chrome web browser crashed (if it crashes in the future). Because debugging software means trying to figure out every possible combination of tasks, it is never possible to come up with every combination unless Google has visibility into how people like you are using the software in the real world. The information that is sent to Google is not shared with anyone and is kept private and confidential so you will not suddenly start receiving spam emails after Google has received your information.

17. Touch to change the size of text displayed on web pages (text scaling) and to override a website's ability to prevent zooming.

18. Touch to change content settings like accepting cookies and sharing your location.

19. Touch to enable or disable accepting cookies.

20. Touch to enable or disable allowing websites to access your location.

21. Touch to enable or disable the ability for Chrome to run JavaScript. This is normally left on as many websites use JavaScript to enhance their site and make it easier to use.

22. Touch to enable or disable blocking web pop-ups.

23. Touch to browse settings for all websites you have visited so that you can clear any data stored by those individual websites and enable or disable sending your GPS location per website.

24. Touch to return to the main Settings screen.

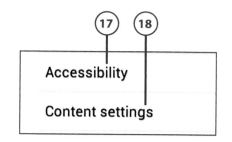

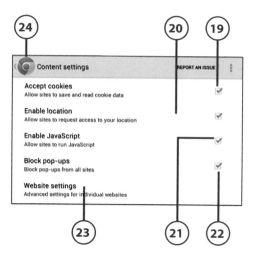

25. Touch Bandwidth Management to enable or disable web page preloading. When enabled, Chrome predicts what links you are likely to click on a web page and preloads them in the background.

26. Touch to enable or disable developer tools such as tilt scrolling and debugging Chrome via USB cable.

27. Touch to save your changes and return to the Chrome main screen.

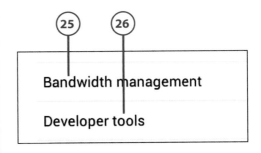

What Is Text Scaling?

When you use text scaling, you instruct your Google Nexus Tablet to always increase or decrease the font sizes used on a web page by a specific percentage. For example, you can automatically make all text 150% larger than was originally intended.

What Are Cookies?

Cookies are small files that are placed on your tablet by websites. They contain information in them that might enhance your browsing experience if you return to their website. For example they could contain information about what pages you visited before, and your browsing history on the website. When you return to the website that placed the cookie, it can read the information in the cookie. Cookies can contain any kind of information so they can be used maliciously, although it's not likely.

How Does Pop-Up Blocking Work?

When you enable pop-up blocking, your Google Nexus Tablet automatically blocks any website request to pop up a window. This is good because almost every pop-up on a website is some kind of scam to get you to touch a link in that pop-up window so that you go to a new site. Sometimes, though, pop-ups are legitimate, and a website that needs you to allow pop-ups will ask you to allow them. You can disable the pop-up blocker anytime and then re-enable it when you stop using that website. Unlike desktop computers, you cannot temporarily stop blocking pop-ups, so you need to remember to manually disable and enable the pop-up blocker.

Click an Email Address to Send an Email

If you see an email address on a web page, touch it to compose a new email to that email address automatically.

Choose which email app to use

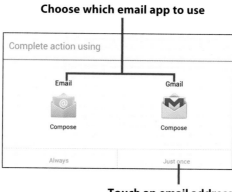

Touch an email address

Add a Phone Number to Contacts

If you see a phone number on a web page, touch it to add it to your Contacts.

Touch a phone number

Touch to add to your contacts

Take Actions on a Link

If you touch and hold a link on a website, you can choose to open it in a new tab, open it in an Incognito tab (secretive browsing), copy the link's address (to paste into another app, such as an email you are composing), and save the link (and its associated web page) as a file on your tablet.

Touch and hold a link

Choose your action

Search Google

See your flight information

**American Airlines
flight 204**

Status: Landed / Sun, Aug 19, 2012

Depart Los Angeles
LAX 9:50 PM (9:55 PM)
Terminal 4, Gate 47A

Arrive Orlando
MCO 5:45am, Mon, Aug 20
Terminal A, Gate 14

1 Final
8/19/2012 4

Red Sox Yankees

Recap & Highlights

Box score

New York

In this chapter, you find out how to use Google Maps, Navigation, and Google Now. Topics include the following:

- → Google Maps
- → Navigation
- → Google Now
- → Taking Map data offline

Google Now and Navigation

You can use your Google Nexus Tablet as a GPS Navigation device while you are walking or driving around. Your tablet also includes a new app called Google Now that provides you all the information you need when you need it.

Google Now

You can access Google Now from the lock screen or from any screen and allows you to search the Internet. Google Now provides you with information such as how long it will take to drive to work and the scores from your favorite teams.

Access Google Now

Before you even unlock your tablet, you can access Google Now by sliding the lock icon up to the word Google. You can also access Google Now from any screen, including the lock screen, by swiping from the bottom bezel up onto the screen and toward the word Google.

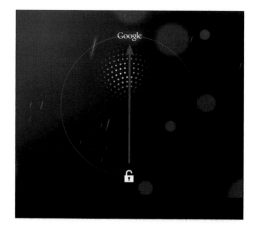

Lock screen: Swipe up from the bottom bezel

Swipe up from the bottom bezel

1. Touch and speak a request or type a search term.

2. Cards relevant to your search or request appear.

3. Cards also automatically appear based on your settings. Examples of these alerts are scores for games the sports teams you follow played recently, upcoming meetings, weather in the location where you work, traffic on the way to work, and others that may be added in the future.

Setting Up Google Now

For Google Now to work for you, you should set it up correctly. This means you need to set up Google Now, but you also have to set up Google Maps, which is used heavily by Google Now.

1. Touch the Menu button.

2. Touch Settings.

3. Touch Google Now.

4. Touch to change how Google Now shows you weather information. You can change when the card appears, where it must show you weather, and the units to use.

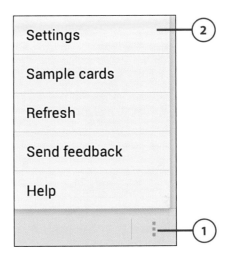

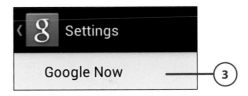

5. Touch to change how Google Now shows you traffic information. You can change when the card appears, the mode of transportation (for example, public transportation or driving), and if it should appear for normal traffic or only for heavy traffic.

6. Touch to change how Google Now shows meeting information. You can change when the card appears (for example for every meeting or only ones that are far away).

7. Touch to change how Google Now shows travel information. For example, you can have it only appear if the place you are travelling to uses a different language.

8. Touch to change how Google Now shows flight information.

9. Touch to change how Google Now shows public transit information.

10. Touch to change how Google Now shows nearby places as you travel.

11. Touch to change how sports team information is shown and when.

12. Touch to choose the ringtone that is played when Google Now needs to alert you.

13. Touch to choose whether you want to feel a vibration when Google Now alerts you.

14. Touch to save your changes and return to the main settings screen.

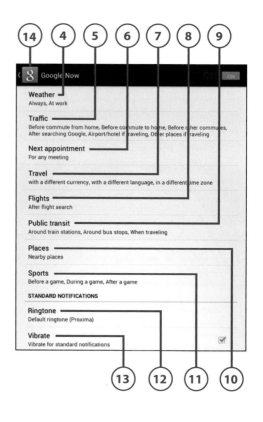

15. Touch Voice.

16. Touch to choose the language that Google Now uses.

17. Touch when you can speak to Google Now. Your choices are Always or only when you are using a hands-free device.

18. Touch to block or allow offensive words to be spoken when search results are returned by voice.

19. Touch to enable or disable Hotword Detection. When enabled, Google Now is always listening for you to say the word Google and it then launches voice search. As of the writing of this book the feature doesn't work.

20. Touch to download speech recognition software so you can do voice searches even when you're not connected to the Internet. You can download multiple languages.

21. Touch to save your changes and return to the main Settings screen.

22. Touch to choose which apps installed on your tablet are searched when you do a search in Google Now.

23. Touch to save your changes and return to Google Now.

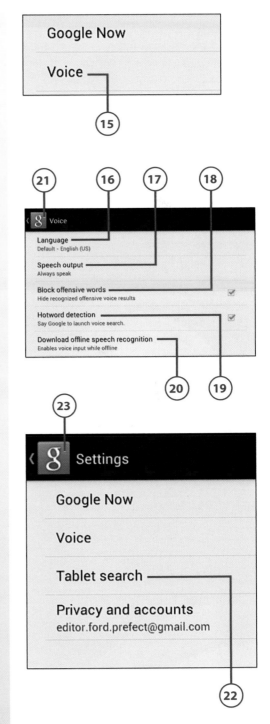

Setting Up Google Maps

Because Google Now relies heavily on Google Maps, you need to change a few things in Google Maps and tell Google Maps where you live and work.

1. Touch to launch Google Maps.

2. Touch the Menu button.

3. Touch My Places.

4. Touch Starred.

5. Touch and hold to enter your home address.

6. Touch and hold to enter your work address.

7. Touch to close the My Places screen.

Maps

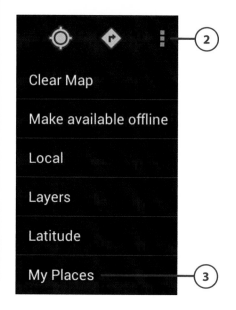

Clear Map

Make available offline

Local

Layers

Latitude

My Places

My Places ✕

OFFLINE STARRED RECENT

Home
2674 Wildberry Ct, Edison, NJ 08817

Work
504 Battery Ave, Brooklyn, NY 11228

8. Touch the Menu button.

9. Touch Settings.

10. Touch Location Settings.

11. Make sure that Enable Location History is enabled (checked).

12. Touch to save your changes and return to the previous screen.

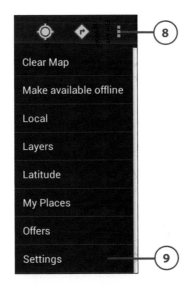

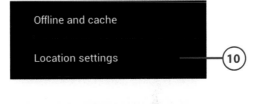

Google Maps

Google Maps enables you to see where you are on a map, find points of interest close to you, give you driving or walking directions, and provide extra layers of information, such as a satellite view.

1. Touch to launch Google Maps.

2. Touch to type a search term.

3. Touch to speak a search term.

4. Touch to get walking or driving directions from one location to another. You can also choose to use public transit or biking paths to get to your destination.

5. Touch the Menu button to see more options.

6. Touch to choose a part of the global map to make available offline. Read more about this later in the chapter in the "Using Offline Google Maps" section.

7. Touch to find local restaurants, coffee shops, bars, and attractions. This menu item also shows you special offers that are being advertised in the area.

8. Touch to add layers to the map view. These can be restaurants, offers, traffic, a satellite view, transit lines, biking paths, and Wikipedia entries for the area.

9. Touch to show your location on the map using Google Latitude, and also see locations of your friends who are using Latitude and sharing their location.

10. Touch to edit your places, such as where you work or where you live, places you have checked into, and places you have recently visited.

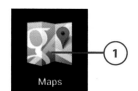

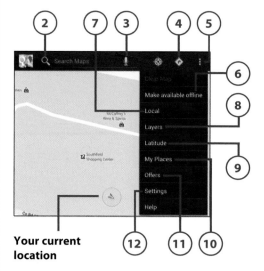

Your current location

11. Touch to see all places that have special offers in the area.

12. Touch to change the settings for Google Maps.

Getting Directions

You can use Google Maps to get directions to where you want to go.

1. Touch the Directions icon.

2. Touch to set the starting point or leave it as My Location (which is where you are now).

3. Touch to choose a location from your Contacts, My Places, or a point on the map.

4. Type in the destination address.

5. Touch to choose a location from your Contacts, My Places, or a point on the map.

6. Touch to flip the start and end points.

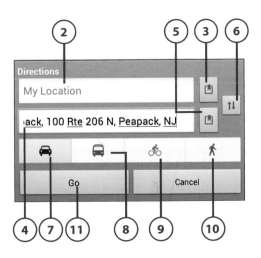

7. Touch to use driving directions.

8. Touch to use public transportation.

9. Touch to use bike paths (if available).

10. Touch to walk to your destination.

11. Touch to see the directions.

12. Touch to change the method to get to your destination.

13. Touch to launch the Navigation app to provide spoken turn-by-turn directions to your destination.

Public Transportation

If you choose to use public transportation to get to your destination, you have two extra options to use. You can choose the type of public transportation to use, including bus, subway, train, or tram/light rail. You can also choose the best route (fewer transfers and less walking).

Extra public transportation options

Google Maps Settings

1. Touch the Menu button.

2. Touch Settings.

3. Touch Display to tweak what is shown on the map. For example you can change the bubble that appears above a landmark to show Navigation, Call, or Street View instead of the standard Get Directions.

4. Touch to remove all map cache. This forces Google Maps to re-download new map areas as needed.

5. Touch to switch to another Google account to use Google Maps.

6. Touch to change your Google Map location setting.

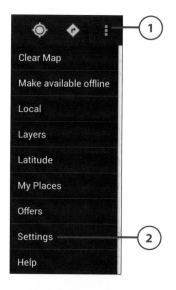

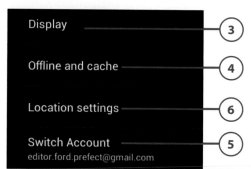

7. Touch to change how Google Maps knows where you are. You can leave it as Detect Your Location (meaning Google Maps uses your GPS location information) or change it to a specific address.

8. Touch to enable or disable reporting your location from your tablet. Combined with the next setting, you can update your location automatically so your friends can see where you are.

9. Touch to enable sharing your location with your friends. You establish which friends see your location in the next step.

10. Touch to manage which of your friends see where you are.

11. Touch to enable location history where Google Maps keeps track of where you have been. Having this enabled makes Google Now much better.

12. Touch to have Google Maps automatically check you in to places you visit and have designated as places you visit a lot.

13. Touch to enable check-in notifications that allow Google Maps to suggest places to visit based on where you are.

14. Touch to manage your places which includes places you check into often and places you want muted (or do not want to hear about).

15. Touch to save your changes and return to the previous screen.

Using Offline Google Maps

Google Maps enables you to download small parts of the global map to your tablet. This is useful if you are travelling and need an electronic map but cannot connect to a network to download it in real-time.

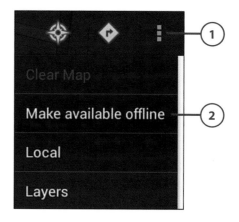

1. Touch the Menu button.

2. Touch Make Available Offline.

3. Pinch to zoom out.

4. Move the blue selection square over the area you want to take offline. This area can be anywhere on the globe.

5. Touch Done to start downloading the map data to your tablet.

How Much Map Can I Take Offline?

When selecting the area of the map to take offline, you are limited to about 100 Mb of map data. You don't need to worry about the size of the data because on the screen, if you have selected an area that is too large, you are warned on the screen.

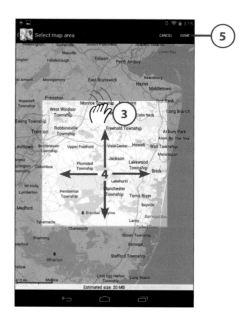

Your selection area is too large warning

It's Not All Good

Offline Maps Have Limited Use

If you download some map data to your tablet, you can use it to zoom in and out of the area you downloaded, and also see where you are on the map in real time all while you have no network coverage. You cannot, however, get directions within the downloaded map area or use the Navigation app to get turn-by-turn directions. You also cannot search for things in the downloaded map area or see points of interest.

So how useful is having map data already downloaded to your tablet? It is useful to a point because it provides an electronic map while offline, but you do need a network connection for directions and navigation to be most useful. Because offline maps are already downloaded, though, they help when you have a network connection and are getting driving directions because Google Maps does not need to download the map data in real time, which could save you a lot of money in data roaming charges.

Navigation

The Navigation app provides the same functionality as built-in car navigation systems or portable navigation units you can buy and stick to your windscreen. Combined with a good window mount, the Navigation app provides the same functionality as other navigation systems.

1. Touch to launch Navigation.

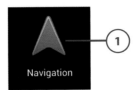

2. Touch to type destination.

3. Touch to speak a destination.

4. Touch to select an address from one of your Contacts.

5. Touch to select an address from places you have starred (marked as favorites).

6. Drive your car and listen to the audible turn-by-turn navigation instructions until you reach your destination.

7. Touch to adjust the route preferences and find alternative routes.

8. Touch to see the entire route as a list.

9. Touch to change the Navigation app settings.

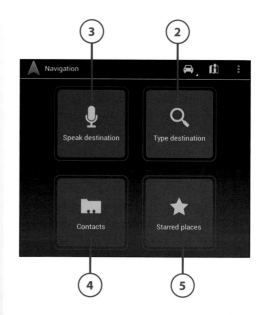

10. Touch to add or remove layers from the navigation view. These include satellite view, traffic, parking, gas stations, ATMs/banks, and restaurants.

11. Touch to turn off the voice prompts.

12. Touch to exit navigation.

13. Touch to search for another destination (this takes you out of the Navigation app and into Google Maps).

14. Touch to set a new destination.

15. Touch to enable screen dimming between direction prompts to save the battery.

Touch to see Day,
Week, and Month views

Touch to add a
new appointment

In this chapter, you find out how to set the time, use the Clock application, and use the Calendar application. Topics include the following:

→ Synchronizing to the correct time
→ Working with the Clock application
→ Setting alarms
→ Working with the Calendar

Working with Date, Time, and Calendar

Your Google Nexus Tablet has a Clock application that you can use as a bedside alarm. The Calendar application synchronizes to your Google or corporate calendars and enables you to create meetings while on the road and to always know where your next meeting is.

Setting the Date and Time

Before you start working with the Clock and Calendar applications, you need to make sure that your Google Nexus Tablet has the correct date and time.

1. Touch Settings.

2. Touch Date & Time.

3. Touch to enable or disable synchronizing time and date with the Internet. It is best to leave this enabled.

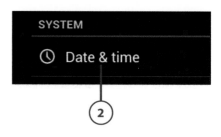

Does Network Time Sync Always Work?

Your tablet updates its clock from the Internet, so as long as you have a Wi-Fi connection and your time zone correctly selected, your clock should stay up to date. If you don't connect to the Internet for a long time, don't worry; your clock remains accurate within a second or two.

4. Touch to choose your time zone.

5. Touch to enable or disable the use of 24-hour time format. This makes your Google Nexus Tablet represent time without a.m. or p.m. For example 1:00 p.m. becomes 13:00.

6. Touch to change the way in which the date is represented. You can leave it set to Regional which allows your tablet to modify how the date is displayed based on the region you are in (using your GPS location), or you can manually set it.

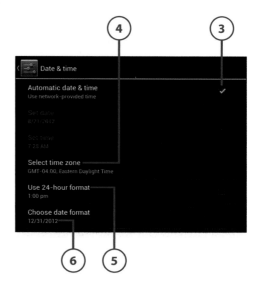

Clock Application

The Clock application is preinstalled on your Google Nexus Tablet and provides the functionality of a bedside clock and alarm clock.

Navigating the Clock Application

1. Touch the Clock icon.

2. Touch to set or edit alarms.

3. Rotate your Google Nexus Tablet onto its side to increase the size of the digits.

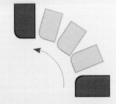

4. Touch and hold to dim the brightness of the screen and put the clock into Night Mode.

5. Touch to add time for another city.

6. Touch to use the Timer function.

7. Touch to use the Stopwatch function.

Time in another city

Managing Alarms

The Clock application enables you to set multiple alarms. These can be one-time alarms or recurring alarms. Even if you exit the Clock application, the alarms you set still trigger.

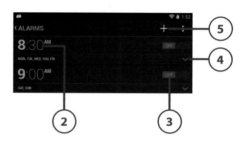

1. Touch to manage alarms.

2. Touch to change an existing alarm's trigger time.

3. Touch to enable or disable an existing alarm.

4. Touch to view or edit an existing alarm's settings, such as whether it repeats, and what sound plays when it triggers.

5. Touch to add a new alarm.

Adding an Alarm

1. Touch to add a new alarm.

2. Use the number pad to enter the time the alarm will trigger.

3. Touch AM or PM.

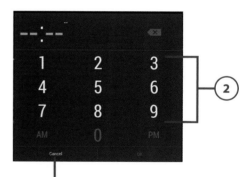

Touch to cancel any changes

4. Touch OK.

5. Touch to make the alarm repeat, and which days it will repeat on.

6. Touch to add a title for your alarm. For example you could call it "Work time!"

7. Touch to change the sound that plays when the alarm triggers.

8. Touch ALARMS to save your changes and return the Clock main screen.

Editing an Alarm

1. Touch to add a new alarm or touch to edit an existing alarm.

2. Touch to enable or disable the alarm.

3. Touch to change the time the alarm will trigger.

4. Touch to edit the alarm's other settings.

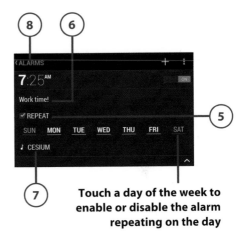

Touch a day of the week to enable or disable the alarm repeating on the day

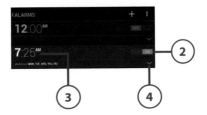

5. Touch to make the alarm repeat, and which days it will repeat on.

6. Touch to change the sound that plays when the alarm triggers.

7. Touch ALARMS to save your changes and return to the main Clock screen.

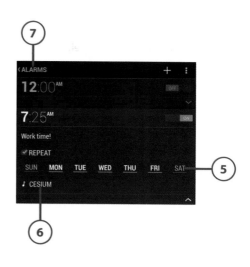

Clock Settings

Use the Settings to control how all alarms function.

1. Touch the Menu button and touch Settings.

2. Touch to change the clock style from digital to analog.

3. Touch to set the volume for all alarms.

4. Touch to set the duration of the snooze period. Your choices range between 5 and 30 minutes.

5. Touch to set how long the alarm plays before it automatically silences itself. Your choices range from 5 minutes to 30 minutes; alternatively you can set it to off so that the alarm plays until you wake up and dismiss it.

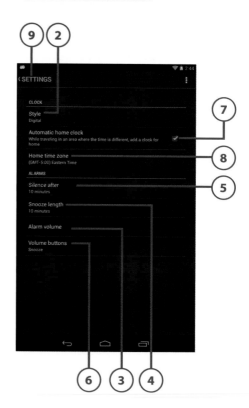

6. Touch to set how the volume buttons behave if you press either of them when the alarm sounds. Your choices are Snooze and Dismiss.

7. Touch to enable or disable the feature that allows the Clock app to automatically add a new clock for your home area when you are travelling.

8. Touch to change your home area time zone.

9. Touch to save the settings and return to the Clock main screen.

Using the Calendar Application

The Calendar application enables you to synchronize all your Google Calendars under your primary Google account to your Google Nexus Tablet. You can accept appointments and create and modify appointments right on your phone. Any changes are automatically synchronized wirelessly back to your Google Calendar.

The Calendar Main Screen

The main screen of the Calendar app shows a one-day, one-week, or one-month view of your appointments. The Calendar app also shows events from multiple calendars at the same time.

1. Touch the Calendar icon.

2. Swipe left to go backward in time.

3. Swipe right to go forward in time.

4. Touch to show today's date.

5. Touch to choose the calendar view. You can choose from the month, week, day, and agenda views.

6. Touch the Menu button for Calendar app actions.

7. Touch to search the calendar for an event.

8. Touch to create a new event.

9. Touch to manually refresh the calendar view.

10. Touch to hide the bottom portion of the screen that shows the full month and list of calendars.

11. Touch to change the Calendar app settings.

12. Touch a calendar to show or hide it. When it is hidden, all events from that calendar are not visible.

13. Touch a day in the month view to quickly jump to that week in the main week view.

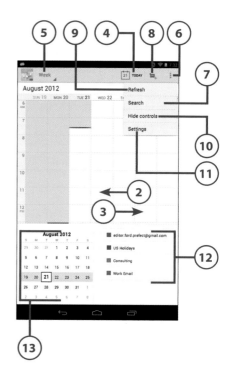

Event Colors

The Calendar app can display one calendar or many calendars at the same time. If you choose to display multiple calendars, events from each calendar are color coded so you can tell which events are from which calendar.

Past and Future

As you look at the different calendar views you see some areas shaded in gray whereas others are shaded white. Gray indicates the past, and white indicates the future.

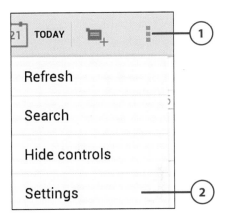

Calendar Settings

In this section you find out how to tweak the calendar app and how to choose which calendars are synchronized to your tablet.

1. Touch the Menu button.

2. Touch Settings.

3. Touch General Settings.

4. Touch to enable or disable hiding events that you have declined.

5. Touch to enable or disable showing the week number. For example, March 26th is in week 13.

6. Touch to set the first day of your week. You can choose Saturday, Sunday, or Monday. You can also choose Locale Default so that the locale you have set in the device settings determines what the first day of the week is. Please see Chapter 9, "Customizing Your Google Nexus Tablet," for more information on setting the device locale.

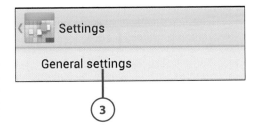

7. Touch to enable or disable using your home time zone when displaying the calendar and event times. When this is enabled, your home time zone is always used even when you are not travelling in it.

8. Touch to set your home time zone if you enabled Use Home Time Zone in Step 7.

9. Touch to clear any calendar searches that you have previously performed.

10. Touch to enable or disable notifications for calendar events.

11. Touch to choose the ringtone to play when you are being alerted for calendar events.

12. Touch to enable or disable a pop-up notification to also be displayed when you are being notified of a calendar event. This pop-up window displays over any app that you are currently using.

13. Touch to set the default event reminder time.

14. Touch to edit your Quick Responses.

15. Touch to save your changes and return to the main settings screen.

16. Touch an account to choose which of its calendars synchronize to your Google Nexus Tablet.

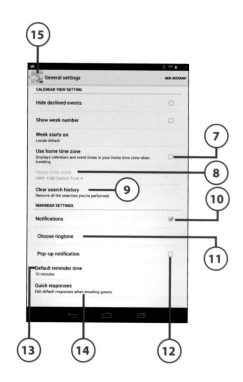

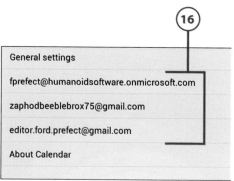

What Are Quick Responses?

Let's say that you are running late for a meeting. When the meeting reminder appears on your tablet and you know that you are running late, you can choose to use a predefined Quick Responses such as "Be there in 10 minutes" or "Go ahead and start without me." When you choose a Quick Response, your tablet emails that response to all meeting participants. See how to use Quick Responses in the next section.

17. Select which calendars in the selected account must synchronize to your tablet.

18. Touch to save your changes and return to the main settings screen.

19. Touch to return to the Calendar app.

Using Quick Response

If you are running late to a meeting, you can send a Quick Response to all meeting participants directly from the meeting reminder.

1. Pull down the Notification Bar.

2. Touch Email Guests.

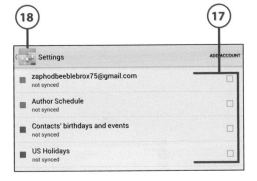

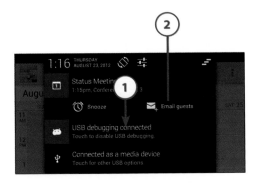

How to Expand an Alert

If you do not see Snooze and Email Guests you can expand the alert by placing your two fingers on the alert and pulling down. Expanding alerts work on all kinds of alerts, including email alerts.

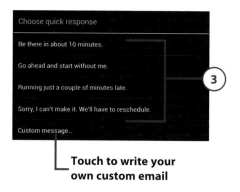

Touch to write your own custom email

3. Touch one of the predefined Quick Responses.

4. Touch the email app from which you want to send the Quick Response.

5. Touch Send.

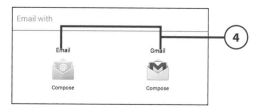

Adding a New Event

While you're on the road you can add a new appointment or event, and you can even invite people to it. Events you add synchronize to your Google and corporate calendars in real time (or when you next connect to a network).

1. Touch to add a new event.

2. Touch to change the calendar to create the event in (if you use multiple calendars) .

3. Touch to enter a title for your event.

4. Enter where the event will take place. This can be a full physical address which is useful because most smartphones and tablets can map the address.

5. Touch to select the start date and time of the event.

6. Touch to select the end date and time of the event.

7. Touch to mark the even as an all day event.

8. Touch to select the time zone the meeting will be held in. This is useful if you will be travelling to the meeting in a different time zone.

9. Enter the event guests or event invitees. As you type names, your Google Nexus Tablet retrieves matching names from your Contacts and your corporate directory.

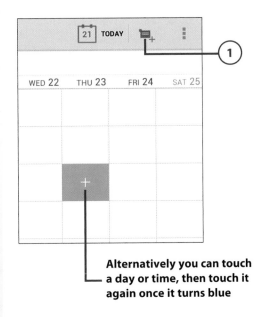

Alternatively you can touch a day or time, then touch it again once it turns blue

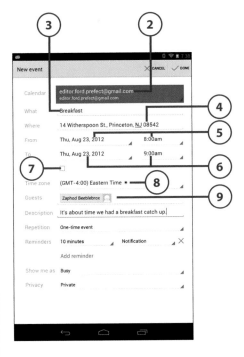

10. Enter a description for the event.

11. Touch to set this as a recurring event. You can make it repeat daily, weekly, or monthly, but you can also set a meeting to repeat—for example, monthly but only every last Thursday.

12. Touch to set how many minutes before the event you are reminded.

13. Touch to set how you are reminded. You can choose to be notified on the device like all other notifications, or via email.

14. Touch to remove a reminder.

15. Touch to add an additional reminder.

16. Touch to choose how to show your availability during this event. You can choose Busy or Available.

17. Touch to choose the privacy of the event. You can choose Public, or make it private so only you can see it. If the event is being created on your corporate calendar, setting it to Private means that people can see you are busy, but cannot see the event details.

18. Touch to save the event. Any attendees that you have added are automatically sent an event invitation.

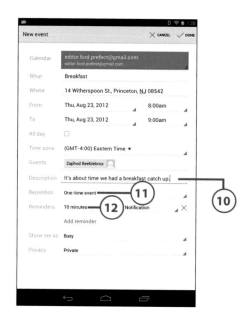

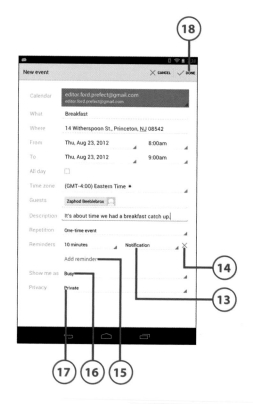

Recurring Events Are Not Flexible

Unfortunately when you choose to make an event repeat, the choices you are given are not flexible. For example, if you want to set up an event that repeats every Thursday, you cannot do this unless you create the event on a Thursday. Let's hope that this is addressed in a future release of Android.

Edit and Delete an Event

To edit or delete a calendar event, touch the event, and either edit the event by touching the pencil icon or delete the event by touching the trash can icon. When you successfully delete an event, the Calendar application sends an event decline notice to the event organizer. You don't have to first decline the meeting before deleting it because this is all taken care of automatically.

Responding to a Gmail Event Invitation

When you are invited to an event, you can choose your response right on your Google Nexus Tablet.

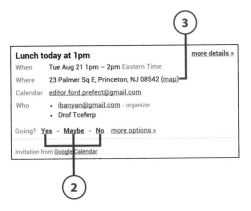

1. Touch to open the event invitation email.

2. Touch Yes, Maybe, or No to indicate whether you will be attending.

3. Touch the event location to have it mapped in Google Maps or another mapping app that you have installed (such as Google Earth).

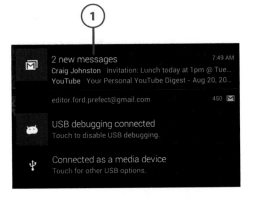

Alternative Event Respond Method

You can also respond to Gmail event invitations directly in the Calendar app. When you receive an event invite in Gmail, it appears in your calendar with an outline. Touch the outlined event to open it and respond.

Responding to a Corporate Event Invitation

When someone invites you to a new event, you receive an email in your corporate inbox with the details of that meeting.

1. Touch to open the event invitation.

2. Touch Invite to see the invitation itself.

3. Touch to view the event invite in the calendar view. This is useful if you want to make sure you don't have a conflict.

4. Touch to choose your response.

Touch to respond

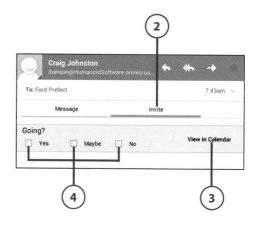

Indicates meeting invite

Alternative Event Respond Method

You can also respond to corporate event invitations directly in the Calendar app. If you receive an event invite in your corporate calendar, it is automatically inserted into the calendar but set as Tentative (Maybe). Touch the event to accept or decline it.

Touch to respond

See your
apps

Search for
apps

In this chapter, you find out how to purchase and use Android applications on your Google Nexus Tablet. Topics include the following:

→ Finding applications with Google Play
→ Purchasing applications
→ Keeping applications up to date

Working with Android Applications

Your Google Nexus Tablet comes with enough applications to make it a worthy tablet. However, wouldn't it be great to play games, update your Facebook and Twitter statuses, or even keep a grocery list? Well, finding these types of applications is what the Google Play is for. Read on to discover how to find, purchase, and maintain applications.

What Happened to Android Market?

Google recently updated the functionality of its store by adding the ability to not only find and purchase Android apps, but also to buy music, buy books, and rent movies. Because of this, Android Market has been renamed to Google Play and sometimes shows as Play Store.

Configuring Google Wallet

Before you start buying applications in the Google Play app, you must first sign up for a Google Wallet account. If you plan to only download free applications, you do not need a Google Wallet account.

1. From a desktop computer or your Google Nexus Tablet, open the web browser and go to http://wallet.google.com.

2. Sign in using the Google account that you use to synchronize email to your Google Nexus Tablet. See Chapter 1, "People (Contacts)," or Chapter 4, "Email," for information about adding a Google account to your Google Nexus Tablet.

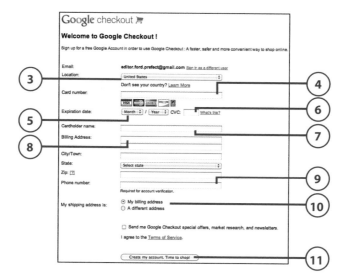

3. Choose your location. If your country is not listed, you have to use free applications until it's added to the list.

4. Enter your credit card number. This can also be a debit card that includes a Visa or MasterCard logo, also known as a check card, so that the funds actually are withdrawn from your checking account.

5. Select the month and year of the card's expiration date.

6. Enter the card's CVC number, which is also known as the security code. This is a three- or four-digit number that's printed on the back of your card.

7. Enter your name.

8. Enter your billing address.

9. Enter your phone number.

10. Although you don't need a mailing address for Google Play, you might want to choose an alternative delivery address for items you purchase from other online stores that use Google Wallet.

11. Click Create My Account when you're done with the form.

Navigating Google Play

Android is the operating system that runs your Google Nexus Tablet and, therefore, any applications that are made for your Google Nexus Tablet need to run on Android. Google Play is a place where you can search for and buy Android applications.

1. Touch the Play application icon.

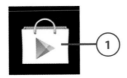

2. Touch the Menu button to see Google Play actions.

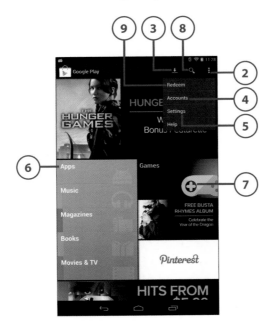

3. Touch to see any apps you have already purchased or downloaded.

4. Touch to select which Google account you want to use when you use the Google Play store, if you have multiple Google accounts.

5. Touch to change the settings for Google Play. See the "Google Play Settings" section later in this chapter for more information.

6. Touch to browse all Android apps.

7. Touch to browse all Android games.

8. Touch to search Google Play.

9. Touch to redeem a Google Play gift card that someone may have purchased for you.

Installing Free Applications

You don't have to spend money to get quality applications. Some of the best applications are actually free.

1. Touch the free application you want to install.

2. Scroll down to read the application features, reviews by other people who installed it, and information on the person or company who wrote the application.

3. Scroll left and right to see the app screenshots.

4. Touch Install to download and install the app.

Tell others about this app

5. Touch to accept the app permissions and proceed with the installation.

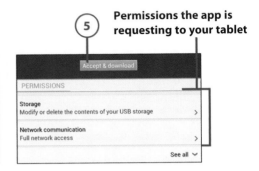

Permissions the app is requesting to your tablet

Beware of Permissions

Each time you download a free app or purchase an app from Google Play, you are prompted to accept the app permissions. App permissions are permissions the app wants to have to use features and functions on your Google Nexus Tablet, such as access to the wireless network or access to your phone log. Pay close attention to the kinds of permissions each app is requesting and make sure they are appropriate for the type of functionality that the app provides. For example, an app that tests network speed will likely ask for permission to access your wireless network, but if it also asks to access your list of contacts, it might mean that the app is malware and just wants to steal your contacts.

Buying Applications

If an application is not free, the price is displayed next to the application icon. If you want to buy the application, remember that you need to already have a Google Checkout account. See the "Configuring Google Checkout" section earlier in the chapter for more information.

1. Touch the application you want to buy.

2. Scroll down to read the application features, reviews by other people who installed it, and information on the person or company who wrote the application.

3. Scroll left and right to see all screenshots and app videos.

4. Touch the price to purchase the app.

5. Touch to change the method of payment or add a new credit card.

6. Touch to accept the terms and conditions of purchase.

7. Touch to purchase the app. You receive an email from the Google Play after you purchase an app. The email serves as your invoice.

What If the Currency Is Different?

When you browse applications in Google Play, you might see applications that have prices in foreign currencies, such as in euros. When you purchase an application, the currency is simply converted into your local currency using the exchange rate at the time of purchase.

Tell others about this app

Permissions the app is requesting to your tablet

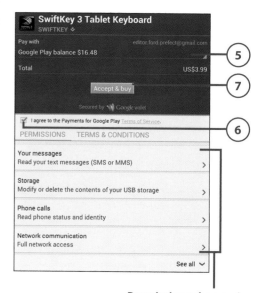

Managing Applications

Use the My Apps section of Google Play to update apps, delete them, or install apps that you have previously purchased.

1. Touch the My Apps icon.

2. Touch All to see all apps that you have installed or might have previously installed.

3. Indicates the app is currently installed.

4. Indicates a free app that you previously installed, but that is no longer installed, or you have not yet installed on this device. Touching the app enables you to install it again for free.

5. Indicates an app you previously purchased and installed, but that is no longer installed, or you have not yet installed on this device. Touching the app enables you to install it again for free.

Touch to see only apps you have installed

Allow an App to Be Automatically Updated

When the developer of an app you have installed updates it to fix bugs or add new functionality, you are normally notified of this in the System Tray so that you can manually update the app. Google Play enables you to choose to have the app automatically updated without your intervention. To do this, open the My Apps screen and touch the app you want to update automatically. Check the box labeled Allow Automatic Updating. Automatic Updating is suspended if the developer of the app changes the permissions that the app requires to function. This allows you to review them and manually update the app yourself.

Uninstalling an App

When you uninstall an app, you remove the app and its data from your Google Nexus tablet. Although the app no longer resides on your Google Nexus tablet, you can reinstall it as described in Step 5 in the previous task because the app remains tied to your Google account.

Touch to uninstall the app

Check to allow automatic updating

Google Play Settings

1. Touch the Menu button.

2. Touch Settings

3. Touch to enable or disable notifications of app or game updates.

4. Touch to enable or disable setting all apps you install to automatically update themselves.

5. Touch to enable or disable an app icon to appear on your Home screen for each app that you install.

6. Touch to clear the Google Play search history.

7. Touch to adjust or set your content filtering level (for example apps for everyone, or apps with medium maturity content, and so on). Use this to filter out apps, movies, music, or books that you deem to be inappropriate.

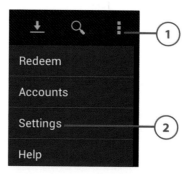

8. Touch to set a PIN that is required before the Google Play User Control settings can be changed (Content Filtering, PIN for purchases, and Set PIN).

9. Touch to use the PIN you set in Step 8 for purchasing apps, music, books or renting movies.

10. Touch to enable or disable having AdMob ads personalized based on your interests. AdMob ads normally show up in Free apps.

11. Touch to return to the main Google Play screen.

Why Lock the User Settings?

Imagine if you buy a Google Nexus Tablet for your child but want to make sure that he doesn't get to any undesirable content. First you set the content filtering to restrict the content visible in Google Play. Next you set the PIN so he can't change that setting. A similar idea goes for limiting purchases.

Touch to enter the PIN before changing the hidden settings

Settings hidden and locked

Accidentally Uninstall an Application?

What if you accidentally uninstall an application or you uninstalled an application in the past but now decide you'd like to use it again? To get the application back, go to the My Apps view in Google Play. Scroll to that application and touch it. Touch Install to re-install it.

Keeping Applications Up to Date

Developers who write Android applications often update their applications to fix bugs or to add new features. With a few quick touches it is easy for you to update the applications that you have installed.

1. If an application you have installed has an update, you see the update notification in the Notification Bar.

2. Pull down the Notification Bar.

3. Touch the update notification.

4. Touch one of the applications that has an update available.

Touch to update all apps at once

5. Touch Update.

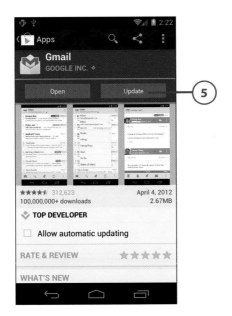

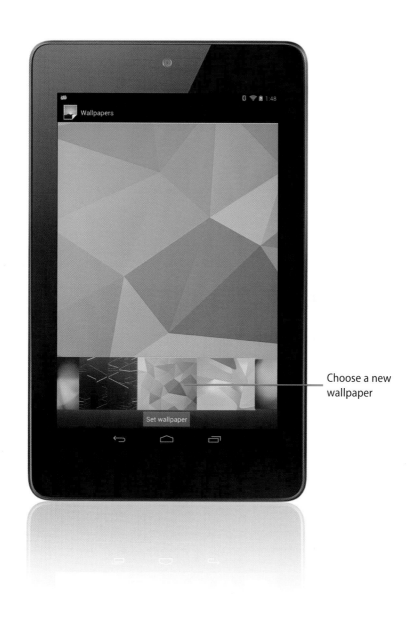

Choose a new wallpaper

In this chapter, you discover how to customize your Google Nexus Tablet to suit your needs and lifestyle. Topics include the following:

→ Using wallpapers and live wallpapers
→ Widgets and Lock Screen Widgets
→ Replacing the keyboard
→ Changing sound and display settings
→ Setting region and language

Customizing Your Google Nexus Tablet

Your Google Nexus Tablet arrives preconfigured to appeal to most buyers; however, you might want to change the way some of the features work, or even personalize it to fit your mood or lifestyle. Luckily your Google Nexus Tablet is customizable.

Changing Your Wallpaper

Your Google Nexus Tablet comes preloaded with a cool wallpaper. You can install other wallpapers, use live wallpapers that animate, and even use pictures in the Gallery application as your wallpaper.

1. Touch and hold on the Home screen.

2. Touch the type of wallpaper you want to use. Use the steps in one of the following three sections to select your wallpaper.

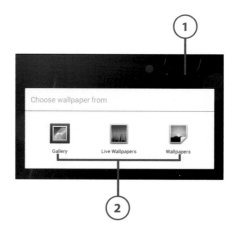

Wallpaper from Gallery Pictures

You can use any picture in your Gallery as a wallpaper.

1. Select the photo you want to use as your wallpaper.

2. Move the crop box to the part of the photo you want to use.

3. Adjust the size of the crop box to include the part of the photo you want.

4. Touch OK to use the cropped portion of the photo as your wallpaper.

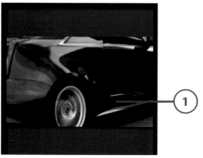

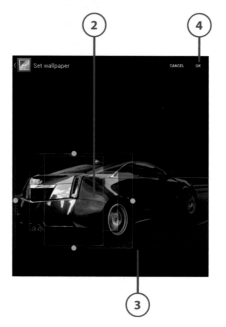

Live Wallpaper

Live wallpaper is wallpaper with some intelligence behind it. It can be a cool animation or even an animation that responds to things such as the music you are playing on your Google Nexus Tablet, or it can be something simple such as the time. There are some very cool live wallpapers in Google Play that you can install and use.

1. Touch the live wallpaper you want to use.

2. Touch to see and change the live wallpaper settings.

3. Touch Set Wallpaper to use the live wallpaper.

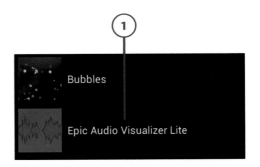

Find More Wallpaper

You can find wallpaper or live wallpaper in Google Play. Open Google Play and search for "wallpaper" or "live wallpaper." Read more on how to use Google Play in Chapter 8, "Working with Android Applications."

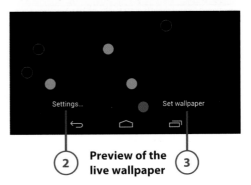

Preview of the live wallpaper

Wallpaper

Choose a static wallpaper.

1. Scroll left and right to see all of the wallpapers.

2. Touch a wallpaper to preview it.

3. Touch Set Wallpaper to use the wallpaper.

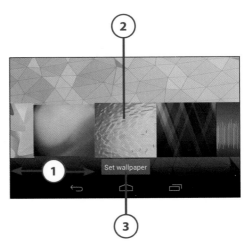

Changing Your Keyboard

If you find it hard to type on the standard Google Nexus Tablet keyboard, or you just want to make it look better, you can install replacement keyboards. You can download free or purchase replacement keyboards from the Google Play. Make sure you install a keyboard before following these steps.

1. Touch Settings.

2. Touch Language & Input.

3. Check the box next to a keyboard you have previously installed (SwiftKey 3 Tablet, in this case) to enable that keyboard.

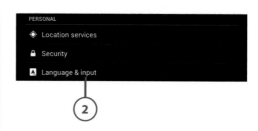

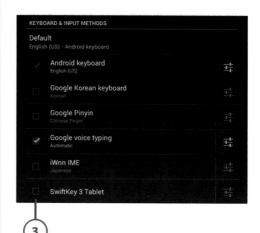

4. Touch OK to change the input method.

Do Your Research
When you choose a different keyboard in Step 3, the Google Nexus Tablet gives you a warning telling you that nonstandard keyboards have the potential for capturing everything you type. Do your research on any keyboards before you download and install them.

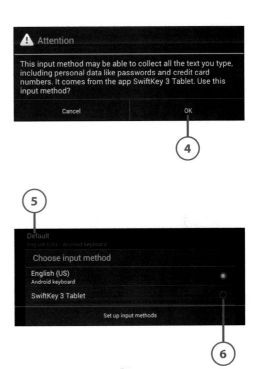

5. Touch Default to change the default keyboard to the one you have just enabled.

6. Touch the name of your new keyboard to select it.

What Can You Do with Your New Keyboard
Keyboards you buy in Google Play can do many things. They can change the key layout, change the color and style of the keys, offer different methods of text input, and even enable you to use an old T9 predictive input keyboard that you may have become used to when using an old "dumb phone" that only had a numeric keypad.

Adding Widgets to Your Home Screens

Some applications that you install come with widgets that you can place on your Home screens. These widgets normally display real-time information such as stocks, weather, time, and Facebook feeds. Your Google Nexus Tablet also comes preinstalled with some widgets. Here is how to add and manage widgets.

Add a Widget

Your Google Nexus Tablet should come preinstalled with some widgets, but you might also have some extra ones that have been added when you installed other applications. Here is how to add those widgets to your Home screens.

1. Touch the Launcher.

2. Touch Widgets.

3. Touch and hold a widget to move it to the Home screen. Keep holding the widget as you move to Step 4

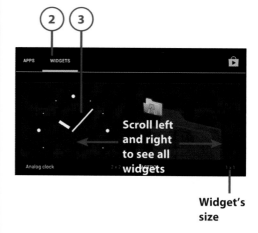

Scroll left and right to see all widgets

Widget's size

4. Position the widget where you want it on the Home screen.

5. Drag the widget between sections of the Home screen.

6. Release your finger to place the widget.

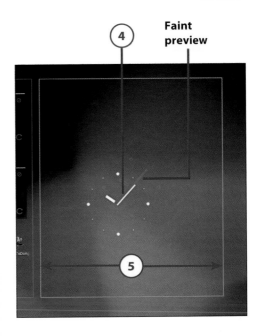

Faint preview

How Many Widgets Can I Fit?

Each part of the Home screen is divided into four blocks across and four blocks down. Notice that each widget shown in the figure for Step 2 shows its size in blocks across and down. From that you can judge if a widget is going to fit on the screen you want it to be on, and the information also helps you position the widget in Step 3.

Remove and Move a Widget

Sometimes you want to remove a widget, resize it, or move it around.

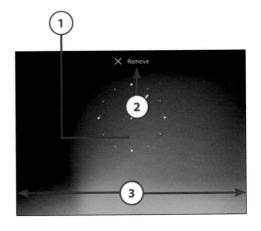

1. Touch and hold the widget until you see a blue shadow, but continue to hold the widget.

2. Drag the widget to the word Remove can to remove it.

3. Drag the widget around the screen or drag it between sections of the Home screen to reposition it.

4. Release the widget.

Resizing Widgets

Some widgets can be resized. To resize a widget, touch and hold the widget until you see a blue shadow and then release it. If the widget can be resized you see the resizing borders. Drag them to resize the widget. Touch anywhere on the screen to stop resizing.

Adding Widgets to Your Lock Screen

Some applications that you install come with widgets that you can place on your Lock screen. Like Home Screen Widgets, these widgets can display real-time information but can be placed on your tablet's lock screen, allowing you to see them before you even unlock your device. Right now the choice of true Android 4.2 Lock Screen widgets is very limited because this feature was just added, but over time, this will improve.

Add a Widget to Your Lock Screen

Your Google Nexus Tablet should come preinstalled with some Lock Screen Widgets, such as the Clock and Gmail apps. Here is how to add those widgets to your Lock screen.

1. Swipe from the Clock widget toward the right on the Lock screen.

2. Touch the plus symbol to add a new widget.

3. Choose a new widget by touching it. In this example, we are choosing the Gmail widget.

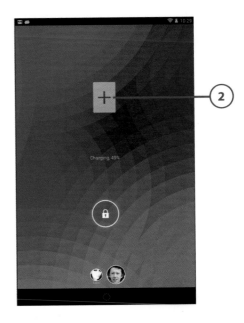

Widget Settings

Some widgets require you to make a decision before they are added. For example, the Gmail lock screen widget asks you which folder you want to display on the lock screen. Here we've chosen the Inbox.

Choose the folder to display

4. The new widget is added.

How Many Widgets Can I Fit?

You can only have one lock screen widget per screen right now.

Remove and Move a Widget

Sometimes you want to remove a widget, or move it around.

1. Touch and hold the widget until the widget shrinks, but continue to hold the widget.

2. Drag the widget to the word Remove to remove it.

3. Drag the widget left and right to reposition it.

4. Release the widget.

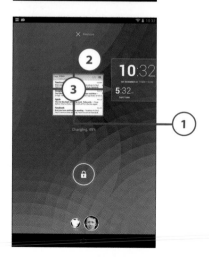

Customizing Language

If you move to another country or want to change the language used by your Google Nexus Tablet, you can do so with a few touches.

1. Touch Settings.

2. Touch Language & Input.

3. Touch Language.

4. Touch the language you want to switch to.

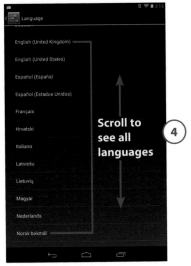

What Obeys the Language Setting?

When you switch your Google Nexus Tablet to use a different language you immediately notice that all standard applications and the Google Nexus Tablet menus switch to the new language. Even some third-party applications honor the language switch. However many third-party applications ignore the language setting on the Google Nexus Tablet. So you might open a third-party application and find that all of its menus are still in English.

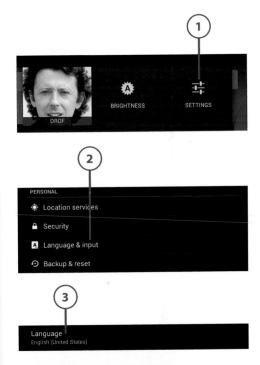

Adjusting Accessibility Settings

Your Google Nexus Tablet includes built-in settings to assist people who might otherwise have difficulty using some features of the device. The Google Nexus Tablet has the ability to provide alternative feedback such as vibration, sound, and even speaking of menus.

1. Touch Settings.

2. Touch Accessibility.

3. Touch to enable or disable TalkBack. When enabled, TalkBack speaks everything, including menus.

4. Touch to enable or disable large text.

5. Touch to enable automatic screen rotation. When disabled, the screen does not rotate between portrait and landscape modes.

6. Touch to enable or disable the feature that causes your tablet speaks your passwords as you type them.

7. Touch to choose which text-to-speech service to use.

8. Touch to change how long you have to hold when you perform a touch and hold on the screen.

9. Touch to allow or disallow Google web scripts that make websites more accessible.

10. Touch to save your settings and return to the previous screen.

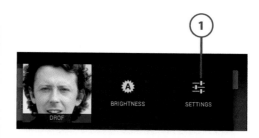

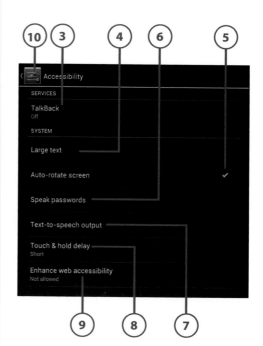

More About Text-To-Speech

By default your Google Nexus Tablet uses the Google Text-To-Speech service to speak any text that you need to read. You can install other text-to-speech software by searching for it in the Google Play store. When it's installed, it shows as a choice for text-to-speech output.

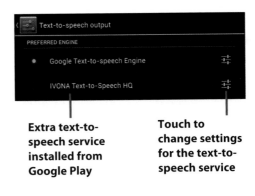

Extra text-to-speech service installed from Google Play

Touch to change settings for the text-to-speech service

Modifying Sound Settings

You can change the volume for games, ringtones, and alarms, change the default ringtone and notification sound, and control what system sounds are used.

1. Touch Settings.

2. Touch Sound.

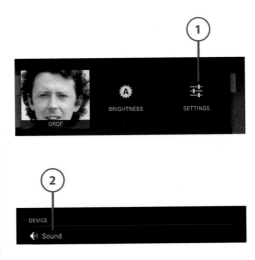

3. Touch to change the volume for games and media such as videos and music, ringtones and notifications, and alarms.

4. Touch to choose the default notification ringtone.

5. Touch to enable or disable the touch sounds that play when you touch something on the screen or a menu.

6. Touch to enable or disable the screen lock sound that plays when your Google Nexus Tablet locks the screen after the inactivity timeout.

7. Touch to save your changes and return to the previous screen.

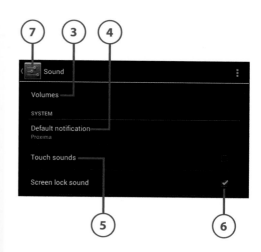

Changing Display Settings

You can change the screen brightness or set it to automatic, change the wallpaper, change how long to wait before your Google Nexus Tablet goes to sleep, the size of the font used, and whether to use the Pulse notification light.

1. Touch Settings.

2. Touch Display.

3. Touch to change the screen brightness manually or set it to automatic. When on automatic, your Google Nexus Tablet uses the built-in light sensor to adjust the brightness based on the light levels in the room.

4. Touch to change the Wallpaper. See more about how to change the wallpaper earlier in this chapter.

5. Touch to choose how many minutes of inactivity must pass before your Google Nexus Tablet puts the screen to sleep.

6. Touch to choose the font size of all text used.

7. Touch to save your changes and return to the previous screen.

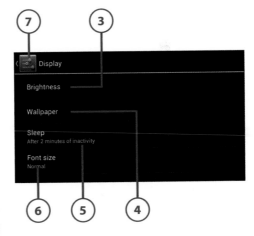

See offers in your area

View your transactions

- → Setting up Google Wallet
- → Using Google Wallet

Google Wallet

Your Google Nexus Tablet has a built-in NFC radio which, among other things, enables you to pay for things like groceries by holding your tablet close to the reader at the checkout counter. Currently in the U.S. you can use Google Wallet to pay for anything in stores where **MasterCard® PayPass™ is accepted.**

Setting Up Google Wallet

Before you can use Google Wallet to wirelessly pay for items at the checkout counter, you need to set it up and select methods of payment.

1. Touch to launch Google Wallet.

2. Touch Get Started.

3. Select an existing Google account to use with Google Wallet.

4. Touch Continue.

5. Touch I Agree to agree to the terms of service.

6. Enter a PIN to secure the Google Wallet app on your tablet.

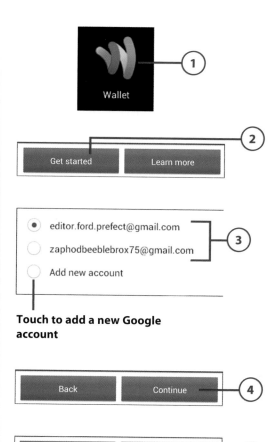

Touch to add a new Google account

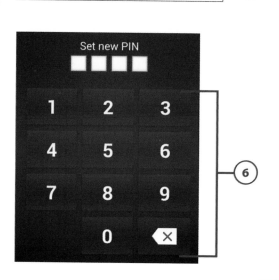

Adding Methods of Payment

Before you can purchase anything using your tablet, you need to add methods of payment. Options include the Google prepaid card, gift cards, or a credit card. By the time you read this book, Google may have eliminated the Google prepaid card.

Add a Google Prepaid Card

1. Touch the Google Prepaid card icon and wait for it to be activated. Once it is activated you will see a $10 credit. This is a free $10 Google gives you to use immediately.

2. Touch the card after it has been activated.

3. Touch to add funds to your Google Prepaid card.

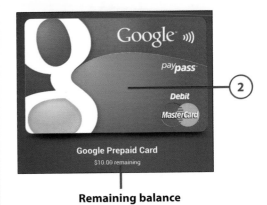

Remaining balance

Add a Credit Card

Perform these steps from the main Google Wallet screen to add a credit card/debit card as a method of payment.

1. Touch Payment Cards.

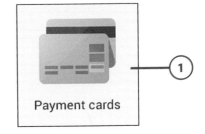

Payment cards

2. Touch to add a new credit or debit card.

3. Enter the information from your credit card.

4. Touch Next to add the card. Your credit card is displayed as a new form of payment.

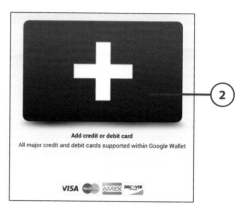

Add credit or debit card
All major credit and debit cards supported within Google Wallet

Add a Gift Card

1. Touch the gift card icon.

2. Touch a gift card type to add information from your gift card.

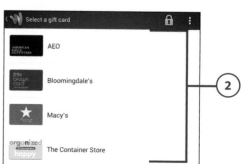

Add gift card

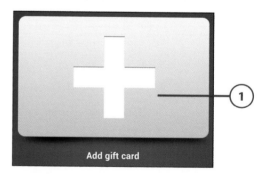

Select a gift card

AEO

Bloomingdale's

Macy's

The Container Store

3. Enter the information from the gift card.

4. Touch Add Card.

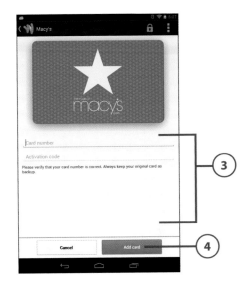

Managing Reward Cards

You can add your store reward cards to Google Wallet so that you can use them at the store without having to carry around the actual physical reward card.

Add a Rewards Card

Right now the Rewards Cards that Google Wallet supports is very limited.

1. Touch Rewards Cards.

2. Touch to add a new rewards card.

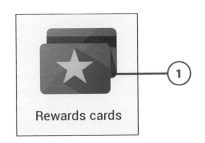

Rewards cards

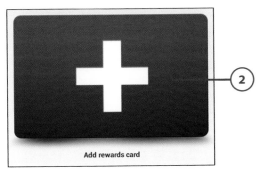

Add rewards card

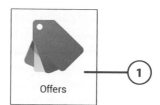

3. Touch a rewards card to add. This example uses Foot Locker VIP.

4. Enter the rewards card number.

5. Touch to add the rewards card to Google Wallet.

Managing Offers

Using Google Wallet you can find and use offers. Offers are anything that a store or restaurant offers free or at a discounted rate when you visit. Traditionally an offer has been a coupon that you have to cut out of a magazine or newspaper and bring to the store or restaurant, but with Google Wallet you can use offers electronically.

Find an Offer

Using Google Wallet you can find offers in your area or at specific stores or restaurants anywhere.

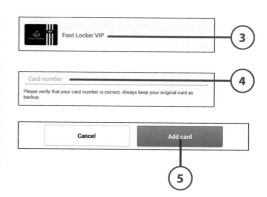

Offers

1. Touch Offers.

2. Touch Find Offers.

3. Touch Save next to an individual offer to save it for later. You can see all your saved offers on the My Offers tab.

Featured offers

My Offers tab

Offer you have already saved

Offers close to you

Use an Offer

When you are at a store you can use a saved offer.

1. Touch My Offers.

2. Touch an offer you want to use at the store.

3. Touch Use Now.

4. Touch Continue and follow the instructions on the next screen.

Redeeming an Offer

When you redeem an offer you have found in Google Wallet, you might be asked to show your tablet to the checkout clerk, or you might be asked to hold your tablet close to the NFC reader at the checkout counter.

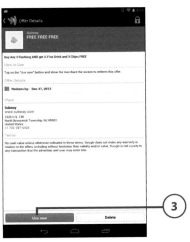

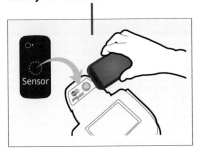

Hand your tablet to the clerk

Show this screen to the retailer to redeem your offer.

Hold your tablet near the reader

Customizing Google Wallet Settings

1. In Google Wallet, touch the Menu button.

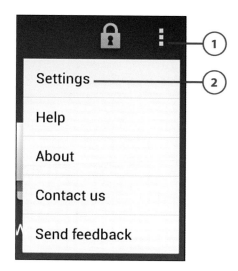

2. Touch Settings.

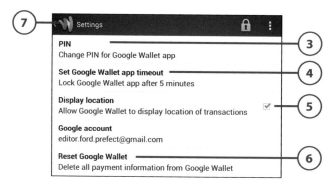

3. Touch to change the four-digit PIN you use to secure Google Wallet.

4. Touch to change how much time must elapse before Google Wallet locks.

5. Touch to enable or disable Google Wallet recording where you are when you make purchases.

6. Touch to delete all payment information from Google Wallet. After you do this, you need to set up your payments methods again

7. Touch to save your changes and return to the previous screen.

Using Google Wallet

After you have Google Wallet set up on your Google Nexus Tablet, you can use it to pay for items at the checkout counter.

1. First make sure that you can use Google Wallet at the checkout counter by looking for these symbols.

**Symbols that indicate you can use
Google Wallet at the checkout counter**

2. When it is time to pay, press the Power button on the side of your tablet to wake it up.

3. Hold your tablet about 1" from the reader that has the symbols shown in the figure for Step 1.

4. You might be prompted to enter your Google Wallet PIN.

5. Remove your tablet from the reader after you hear the confirmation tone.

Touch to buy more books

Touch a book to read it

In this chapter, you find out how to buy books, read books, and subscribe to your favorite magazines. Topics include the following:

→ Buying books

→ Reading books

→ Buying magazine subscriptions

Books and Magazines

This chapter covers how you can use your Google Nexus Tablet for reading books and magazine subscriptions.

Books

The Google Play store has a section that enables you to purchase (and in some cases get free) books in eBook form. After you have an eBook, you can read it at your leisure and even bookmark your favorite pages.

Navigating the Play Books App

The Play Books app enables you to read your books, bookmark pages, and find and purchase more books.

1. Touch to launch Play Books.

2. Touch to find and purchase more books.

3. Touch to search for a book in your library.

4. Touch to see options for the Play Books app.

5. Touch to choose which books you want to make available offline when you know you won't have network coverage.

6. Touch to change the Play Books app settings.

7. Touch a book to read it or continue reading it.

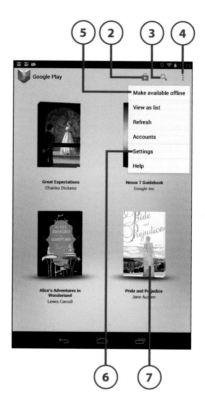

Buying Books

The procedure is the same for downloading a free book and buying a book. The only difference is a free book shows a price of zero.

1. Touch to open the Google Play Books store.

2. Touch a book.

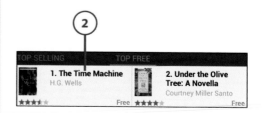

3. Scroll down to read reviews on the book.

4. Touch to share the book with people using Facebook, Twitter, email, and many other methods.

5. Touch to read a free sample of the book for you download it.

6. Touch to download the book.

7. Touch to change the method of payment.

8. Touch to accept and download the free book. If the book is not free, the price of the book is displayed on this screen.

Searching for a Book

Finding books in the Play Store is easy. You can swipe left and right to see different categories of books, such as top free books or recent arrivals, but you can also use the search icon to find books. When you choose to search, remember that you can also speak your searches. One drawback of searching is that your search is done across all stores, so you see related results for apps, movies, TV shows, and books.

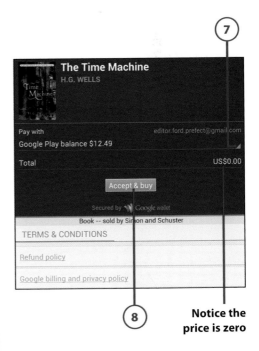

Notice the price is zero

9. Touch to continue shopping for books.

10. Touch to read your book immediately.

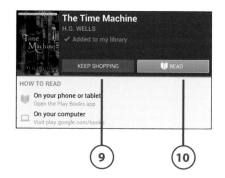

Reading Books

As you read a book, you can bookmark certain pages, jump to different chapters, and even change the font size.

1. Touch a book to open it.

2. Swipe left and right across the screen to flip forward and backward through the book.

3. Touch near the middle of the screen to reveal the controls.

4. Drag left and right to quickly jump to a specific page.

5. Touch to switch between the day and night theme, change the typeface, control the brightness, and increase or decrease the font size.

6. Touch to list all the chapters and bookmarks.

7. Touch to search the entire book for specific text.

8. Touch to add or remove a bookmark, switch between the book's original page layout and flowing text, and change the Play Book app settings.

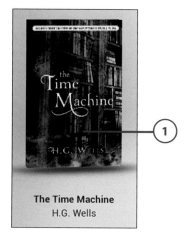

The Time Machine
H.G. Wells

Control the Look

Touch the Font icon to reveal ways to control how the book appears on your screen. The day and night setting switches the text from black text on a white background (day) to white text on a black background (night). You can also change the typeface, text alignment, brightness, line height, and font size.

Adjust the settings to suit your preferences

What Are Original Pages?

When you read a book on your tablet, the app defaults to showing the book using Flowing text. This means that the text of the book is all there, but it's not structured in its original format per page. If you switch to Original pages, you can page through the book as it was originally laid out, using the original typeface and alignment.

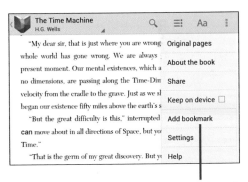

Touch to bookmark the current page

Touch to see a list of bookmarks

Bookmarks

As you read through your book, you might want to bookmark certain pages to come back to later. To do this, touch the middle of the screen to reveal the controls and then touch the Menu button. Touch Add Bookmark. You can also see a list of all of your bookmarks and jump directly to them.

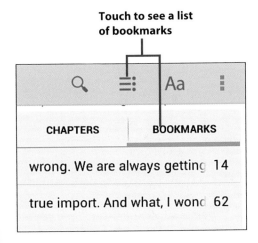

SAVE YOUR BOOK TO YOUR TABLET

When you buy and read a book it isn't actually stored on your tablet—it's in the Google cloud. You need to be connected to Wi-Fi to read your book. If you know that you won't be able to connect (as when you're on a plane), you can copy the book to your tablet. Doing this enables you to read your book even with no connection to the Internet. While you still have network coverage, touch the Menu icon and check the box next to Keep on Device.

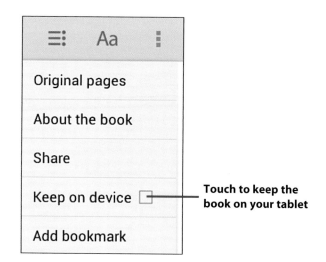

Touch to keep the
book on your tablet

Magazines

You can subscribe to print magazines on your tablet and have them delivered in electronic form to read anytime. The Play Magazines app enables you to subscribe to and read your magazines.

1. Touch to launch the Play Magazines app.

2. Scroll through your magazines.

3. Touch a magazine to open it.

4. Touch to find more magazines and subscribe to them.

5. Touch to download a magazine to your tablet for reading when you're not connected to the Internet.

Reading a Magazine

1. Touch to open a magazine.

Indicates the progress of downloading the magazine

2. Swipe through the magazine pages.

3. Touch to advance through the pages one at a time.

4. Touch to see a list of stories and jump to them.

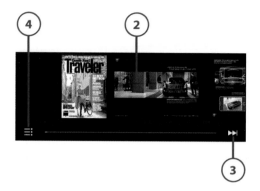

Subscribing to a Magazine

While some magazines are free, most require a subscription. You can choose from a monthly subscription to an annual subscription.

1. Touch the Menu button.

2. Touch Manage Subscriptions.

3. Enter your Google email address.

4. Enter the password for the Google email address.

5. Touch Sign In.

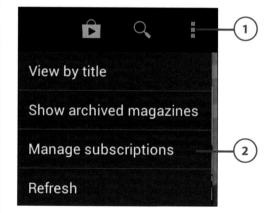

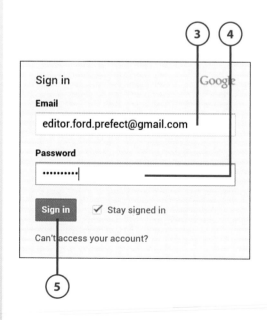

6. Touch one of your magazines or a new one that you have found.

7. Touch Subscribe.

8. Touch to choose a monthly subscription.

9. Touch to choose a yearly subscription.

10. Touch to continue and pay for your subscription.

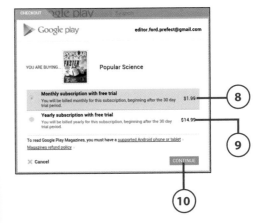

See your battery
usage trends

In this chapter, you find out how to maintain your Google Nexus and solve problems. Topics include the following:

→ Updating Android
→ Optimizing battery life
→ Identifying battery-hungry applications
→ Caring for your Google Nexus Tablet

12

Maintaining Your Google Nexus Tablet and Solving Problems

Every so often Google releases new versions of Android that have bug fixes and new features. In this chapter you find out how to upgrade your Google Nexus Tablet to a new version of Android and how to tackle common problem-solving issues and general maintenance of your tablet.

Updating Android

New releases of Android are always exciting because they add new features, fix bugs, and tweak the user interface. Here is how to update your Google Nexus Tablet.

Update Information

Updates to Android are not delivered on a set schedule. The update messages appear as you turn on your Google Nexus Tablet, and they remain in the Notification Bar until you install the update. If you touch Install Later, your Google Nexus Tablet reminds you that there's an update every 30 minutes. Sometimes people like to wait to see if there are any bugs that need to be worked out before they update, so it is up to you.

1. Pull down the System Bar.

2. Touch System Update Available.

3. Touch Install Now.

4. Touch Restart & Install. Your Google Nexus Tablet updates and reboots.

Manually Check for Updates

If you think there should be an update for your Google Nexus Tablet, but have not yet received the onscreen notification, you can check manually by touching Settings, About Tablet, and System Updates. If there are updates, they are listed on this screen. If not, touch the Check Now onscreen button to check manually.

Indicates a system update is available ① ②

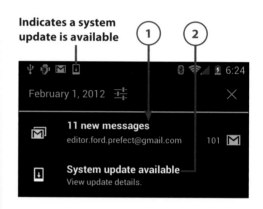

Touch to install later ③

④

Restart & install

Optimizing Battery Life

The battery in your Google Nexus Tablet is a lithium ion battery that provides good battery life when you take care of it. Changing the way you use your Google Nexus Tablet helps prolong the battery's life, which gives you more hours in a day to use your Tablet.

Looking After the Battery

There are specific actions you can take to correctly care for the battery in your Google Nexus Tablet. Caring for your battery helps it last longer.

→ Try to avoid discharging the battery completely. Fully discharging the battery too frequently harms the battery. Instead, try to keep it partially charged at all times (except as described in the next step).

→ To avoid a false battery level indication on your Google Nexus, let the battery fully discharge about every 30 charges. Lithium-ion batteries do not have "memory" like older battery technologies; the battery meter gives a false reading if you don't fully discharge the battery every 30 charges.

→ Do not leave your Google Nexus in a hot car or out in the sun anywhere, including on the beach, as this can damage the battery and make it lose charge quickly. Leaving your Google Nexus Tablet lying in the snow or in extreme cold also damages the battery.

→ Consider having multiple chargers. For example, you could have one at home, one at work, and maybe one at a client's site. This enables you to always keep your Google Nexus Tablet charged.

Determining What Is Using the Battery

Your Google Nexus Tablet enables you to see exactly what apps and system processes are using your battery. Having access to this information can help you alter your usage patterns and reduce the battery drain.

1. Touch Settings.

2. Touch Battery.

3. Touch to manually refresh the display.

4. Touch an app or Android service to see more details about it, including how much time it has been active, how much processor (CPU) time it has used, and how much data it has sent and received (if applicable).

5. Touch the battery graph for more details.

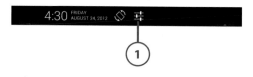

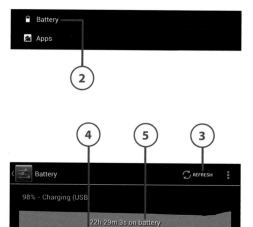

6. GPS On indicates when the GPS radio was being used through the battery graph's time span.

7. Wi-Fi indicates when the Wi-Fi radio was being used through the battery graph's time span.

8. Awake indicates when your Google Nexus Tablet was awake through the battery graph's time span.

9. Screen On indicates when your Google Nexus Tablet's screen was on through the battery graph's time span.

10. Charging indicates when your Google Nexus Tablet was charging through the battery graph's time span.

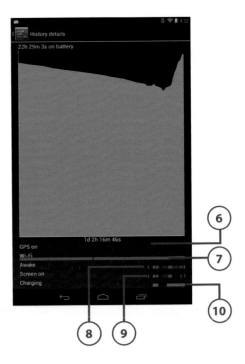

How Can Seeing Battery Drain Help?

If you look at the way your battery has been draining, you can see when the battery was draining the fastest, and you should be able to remember what apps you were using at that time or what you were doing on your Google Nexus Tablet. Based on that you can either change your usage habits or maybe come to the conclusion that a specific app you are using is misbehaving.

Applications and Memory

When applications run on your Google Nexus Tablet, they all run in a specific memory space that is limited to 1GB. Although Android tries to do a good job of managing this memory, sometimes you have to step in and close an app that is consuming too much memory.

1. Touch Settings.

2. Touch Apps.

3. Touch Running to see only apps that are currently running.

4. The graph shows how much memory is being used by running apps and cached processes compared to how much space is free.

5. Touch an app to see more information about it.

6. Touch Stop if you believe the app is misbehaving.

7. Touch to report an app to Google. You might want to do this if it is misbehaving, using up too many resources, or you suspect it of stealing data.

8. Indicates the processes that are being used by this app.

When to Manually Stop an App

After you have been using your Google Nexus Tablet for a while, you'll become familiar with how long it takes to do certain tasks such as typing, navigating menus, and so on. If you notice your Google Nexus becoming slow or not behaving the way you think it should, the culprit could be a new application you recently installed. Because Android never quits applications on its own, that new application continues running in the background and causing your Google Nexus to slow down. This is when it is useful to manually stop an app.

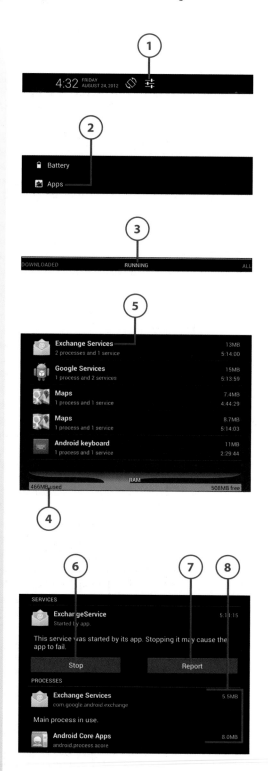

See How Much Data Apps Use

You might want to see how each app consumes data while it's running in the foreground or in the background. You might also want to limit an app's data consumption when it is running in the background.

1. Touch Settings.

2. Touch Data Usage.

3. Touch the Menu button.

4. Touch to enable or disable data auto-sync for all apps (not advisable).

5. Slide the markers to increase or decrease the data measurement period.

6. Touch an app to see more detailed data usage information.

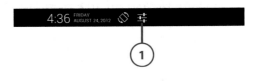

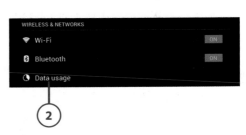

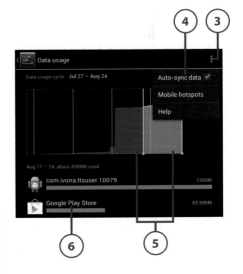

7. Touch to view and change the app's settings.

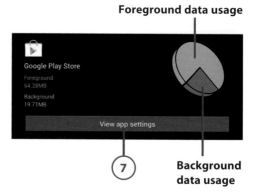

Foreground data usage

Google Play Store

Foreground
64.28MB

Background
19.71MB

View app settings

⑦

Background data usage

Caring for Your Nexus Tablet's Exterior

Because you need to touch your Google Nexus Tablet's screen to use it, it picks up oils and other residue from your hands. You also might get dirt on other parts of the tablet. Here is how to clean your Google Nexus Tablet.

1. Wipe the screen with a microfiber cloth. You can purchase these in most electronic stores, or you can use the one that came with your sunglasses.

2. To clean dirt off other parts of your tablet, wipe it with a damp cloth. Never use soap or chemicals on your Google Nexus Tablet as they can damage it.

3. When inserting the Micro-USB connector, try not to force it in the wrong way. If you damage the pins inside your Google Nexus Tablet, you will not be able to charge it.

Getting Help with Your Google Nexus Tablet

There are many resources on the Internet where you can get help with your Google Nexus Tablet.

1. Visit the Official Google website at http://www.android.com.

2. Check out some Android blogs:

   → Android Central at http://www.androidcentral.com/

   → Android Guys at http://www.androidguys.com/

   → Androinica at http://androinica.com/

3. Contact me. I don't mind answering your questions, so visit my official *My Google Nexus Tablet* book site at http://www.CraigsBooks.info.

Capture panoramas

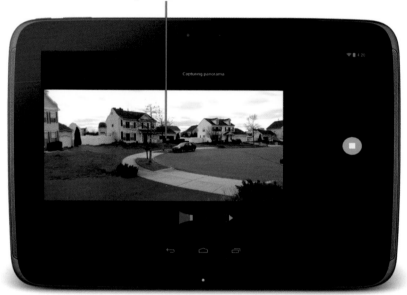

In this chapter, you learn how to take pictures and record video with your Google Nexus 10 Tablet, how to store them, and how to share them with friends. Topics include the following:

→ Using the camera
→ Taking panoramic pictures
→ Recording video
→ Synchronizing pictures
→ Viewing pictures

Taking Pictures and Recording Video

Whereas the Google Nexus 7 Tablet does not have a rear-facing camera, the Google Nexus 10 Tablet has a decent 5 megapixel rear-facing camera with mechanical auto-focus. This means it can take really good pictures. After you take those great pictures, you can share them with friends. You can also synchronize the pictures directly with your computer or using Google Photos in the cloud.

Using the Camera (Nexus 10 Only)

Let's start by looking at the Camera application itself before discussing how to take pictures and record videos. The following steps work for both taking pictures and recording video unless noted.

1. Touch to launch the Camera.

2. Touch to change the camera mode between still camera, panoramic camera, 360 panoramic, and video camera.

3. Touch to change the camera settings. (See the next section for more information about the camera settings.)

4. Touch anywhere in the frame to make the camera focus specifically in the area. The focus ring turns green if it's successful and red if it cannot focus. This only works for regular picture mode.

5. Touch to take a picture.

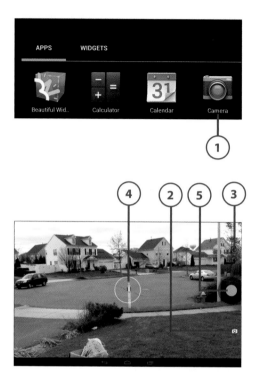

Its Not All Good

Zooming In—Is It Worth It?

Before you snap your picture or record a video (and also while you're recording a video), you can zoom in on the frame. To zoom in, place your thumb and forefinger on the screen and move them apart. To zoom back out, move your thumb and forefinger back together. This is commonly called "pinch to zoom."

When you slide your thumb and forefinger apart to zoom in, the Camera app is faking the zoom. Although the image appears to be getting larger, what is really going on is the image is simply being manipulated to appear like it's zooming in. This is commonly called "digital zoom." Optical zoom is when the camera actually zooms using a lens movement, which is something that this camera cannot do.

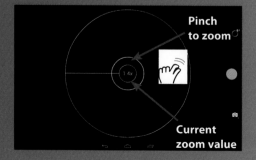

Using Camera Settings

Using camera settings, you can change things such as the resolution of each picture, picture review time, filters, scene mode, white balance, and more. The settings that are not available when you're in video mode are noted in the steps.

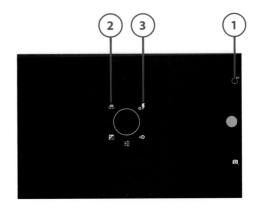

1. Touch to reveal the camera settings.

2. Touch to switch between the front-facing and rear-facing cameras.

3. Touch to set the camera flash mode. The camera flash mode setting is only visible when you have the rear-facing camera selected.

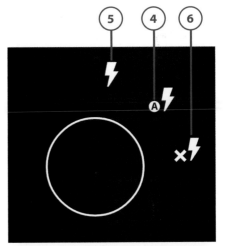

4. Touch to set the flash to Auto, which lets the camera decide when to fire the flash based on the lighting conditions. Auto flash is not available when the camera is in video mode.

5. Touch to set the flash to On. This means the flash is always used regardless of lighting conditions. When in video mode, the flash acts as a permanent light.

6. Touch to set the flash to Off, which means the flash is never used.

7. Touch to set the White Balance.

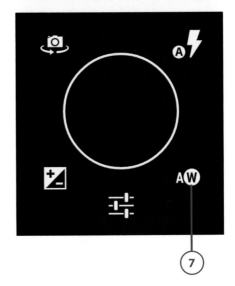

8. Touch to set the White Balance to Auto, which lets the camera decide how to set the White balance.

9. Touch to choose the setting that is appropriate if you are outdoors and it is cloudy.

10. Touch to the setting that is appropriate if you are outdoors and it is sunny.

11. Touch to choose the setting that is appropriate if you are indoors and the main light source is from fluorescent bulbs.

12. Touch to choose the setting that is appropriate if you are indoors and the main light source is incandescent bulbs.

13. Touch to change the exposure setting, which enables you to force the camera to either underexpose or overexpose a picture. Exposure settings are not available when the camera is in video mode.

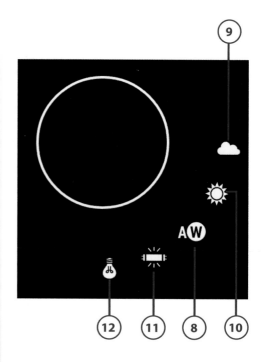

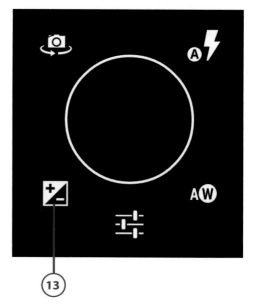

14. Choose positive numbers to overexpose the picture (by keeping the shutter open longer).

15. Choose negative numbers to underexpose the picture (by keeping the shutter open for a shorter period).

16. Touch to change the scene mode or picture size. Also use this option to store your location with the pictures. These settings are specific to the regular camera mode.

17. Touch to adjust the resolution of the picture. The highest is 5 megapixels for the rear-facing camera and 1.3 megapixels for the front-facing camera.

18. Touch to enable or disable storing your geographic location in the picture or video.

19. Touch to change the scene mode. Changing the scene can help the camera adjust itself to the type of scenery and type of picture being taken.

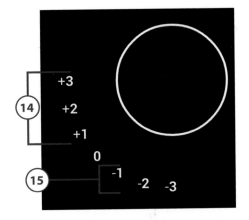

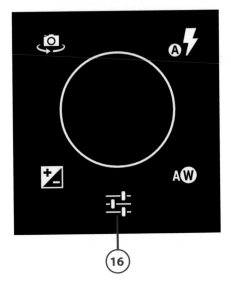

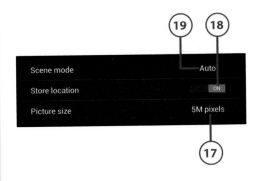

20. Choose a scene like Action or Night, or leave the mode on Auto to let the camera use a setting based on lighting conditions.

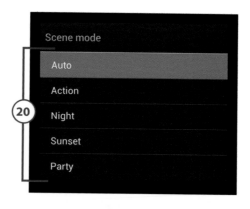

Quicker Way to Change Camera Settings

You can make changes to the camera settings quickly by touching and holding anywhere on the screen and then sliding your finger over the setting you want to change. When you release your finger, the new setting takes effect.

Taking Regular Pictures

Now that you have the settings the way you want them, take a few pictures. You can jump straight to Step 5 and take the picture, but you might want to first set up your shot. Remember to always take pictures in landscape mode for the best results.

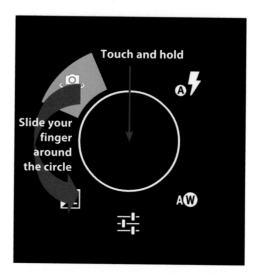

1. Touch the Camera icon.

2. Touch to change the camera mode.

3. Touch to select regular camera mode.

4. Touch the area of the frame you want to focus on specifically. When you release your finger, the camera indicates a green focus ring if it can successfully focus or a red focus ring if it cannot.

5. Touch to take the picture.

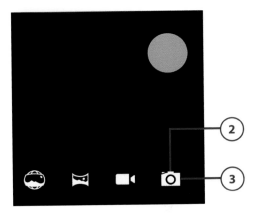

Focus on Parts of a Picture

You can actually focus on a certain part of a scene. By touching the part of the picture you want in focus, you see that the rest of the picture goes out of focus. Using this trick enables you to take some amazing pictures.

Focus ring indicator

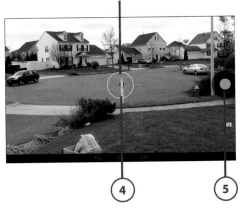

Taking Panoramic Pictures

Your Google Nexus 10 can take panoramic pictures. Panoramic pictures are achieved by taking multiple pictures from left to right or right to left, and stitching them together in one long picture. Luckily your Nexus 10 does all that work for you.

1. Touch the Camera icon.

2. Touch to change the camera mode.

3. Touch to select Panoramic.

4. Touch to start the panorama.

5. Slowly rotate your body from left to right or right to left to capture the panorama. Use the indicator at the bottom of the screen to track your progress.

6. When you have rotated all the way, the camera automatically stitches the pictures together into a panorama and save it.

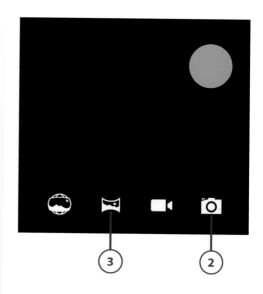

Can You Change the Width of the Panorama?

To create shorter panoramas, instead of rotating all the way from left to right or right to left until the indicator at the bottom of the screen reaches the opposite end, you can touch the blue button to immediately stop the panorama process and save it as is.

Indicates your progress

Moving Too Fast

When you take panoramic pictures, you have to rotate slowly. If you start moving too fast, the camera indicates this to you by changing the progress indicator to red. Slow down when this happens; otherwise the panorama will not look good.

Indicates saving progress

Taking Photo Sphere (360 Panoramic) Pictures

Your Google Nexus 10 can take 360-degree panoramic pictures or Photo Spheres. Photo Sphere pictures are achieved by taking multiple pictures in all directions around you, and stitching them together in one large sphere image.

1. Touch the Camera icon.

2. Touch to change the camera mode.

3. Touch to select Photo Sphere.

4. Move your Nexus 10 until the circle is over the blue dot. After you have done that, wait until you see three white dots appear.

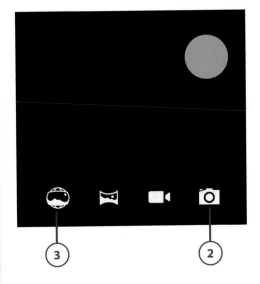

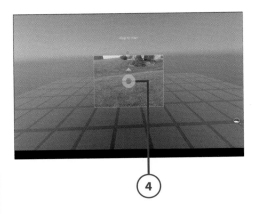

5. Slowly move your Nexus 10 around and guide the circle over the blue dots. Each time you line them up, another image is captured for your Photo Sphere.

6. When you have have captured enough images, touch to stop the Photo Sphere process. The images will be stitched together silently in the background. You will be able to view your Photo Sphere using the Gallery app, which we will cover later in this chapter.

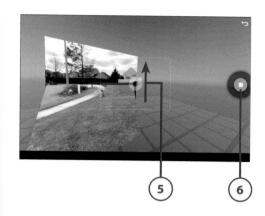

Recording Video

Your Google Nexus 10 can take pictures and record video. When in video mode, the camera even enables you to record time lapse video to capture scenes over long periods of time.

1. Touch to launch the Camera app.

2. Touch to choose the camera mode.

3. Touch to switch to video mode.

4. Rotate your Nexus 10 sideways before recording video.

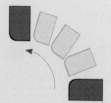

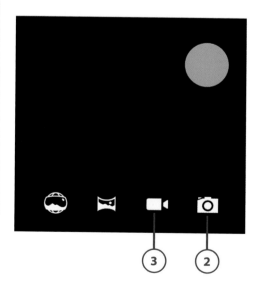

5. Touch to start recording video.

6. Touch to stop recording video.

Elapsed time

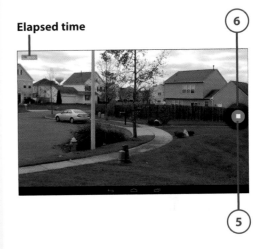

Why Sideways?

All televisions and computer screens use an aspect ratio of 16:9. This means that they are wider than they are tall. If you do not rotate your tablet sideways before recording, when you watch the video on a TV or computer you see a small tall image in the middle of the screen. If you rotate your Nexus 10 on its side, the video that you record is also at 16:9 ratio and will fill the TV and computer screen when you watch it.

Changing Video Settings

Although most of the camera settings were covered in the section "Using Camera Settings" earlier in the chapter, this section covers some settings specific to recording video.

1. Touch to see settings.

2. Touch to see advanced settings.

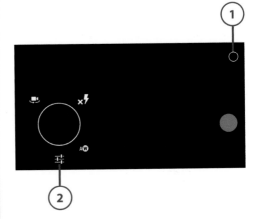

3. Touch to enable or disable storing the GPS coordinates of your location when you record the video.

4. Touch to set the video quality. The three choices are HD 1080p (the best High Definition video), HD 720p (the lower level of High Definition), or SD 480P (video that is similar to regular non-HD television, or Standard Definition).

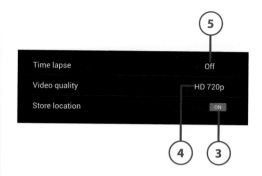

5. Touch to enable time lapse recording and set a video time-lapse interval. Using time lapse means that the video camera records video at set intervals instead of continuously.

6. Touch to enable or disable time lapse mode.

7. Swipe up or down to change between seconds, minutes, and hours.

8. Swipe up and down to change the interval.

9. Touch Done to save your changes.

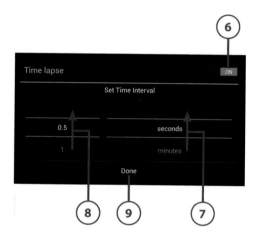

Viewing and Managing Your Photos (Nexus 7 and Nexus 10)

No matter if you have snapped pictures using your Google Nexus 10, or have synchronized photos from a computer, you can use the Gallery application to manage, edit, and share your photos.

Navigating the Gallery

1. Touch to launch the Gallery application.

2. Touch a thumbnail photo to open an album.

3. Touch to reorder the way the photos are displayed. Instead of displaying them by the album they are in, you can display photos grouped by locations, times, people, and tags.

4. Swipe left and right to see all photo albums.

5. Touch to launch the Camera app. This icon is not available on the Nexus 7.

6. Touch the photos labeled as Camera to see pictures taken on your Galaxy Nexus. This album is not available on the Nexus 7.

7. Touch the Menu button to see Gallery app actions.

8. Touch to choose which photos are available offline. See more about moving photos offline later in this chapter.

9. Touch to manually refresh the Gallery view. This is helpful to update the view after very recently uploading photos to Google from your computer.

10. Touch to change the Gallery app settings.

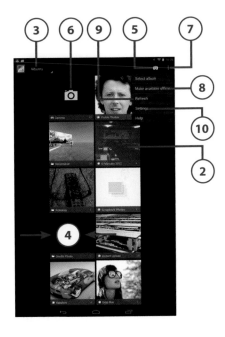

Deleting Photo Albums

You can delete one or many photo albums, but only if they were created on your Nexus Tablet. Albums created on your desktop computer that you can also see on your Nexus Tablet cannot be deleted.

1. Touch and hold a photo album.

2. Touch to select additional albums if you want to.

3. Touch to delete the album(s).

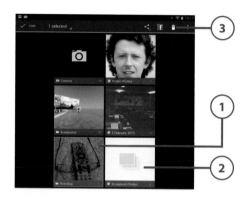

Opening Photo Albums

After you open a photo album, you can manage the photos in it, edit them, and share them.

1. Touch an album to see all pictures in it.

2. Touch the Menu button to see more options.

3. Touch to see a slide show of all the photos in the album.

4. Touch Group By to group the photos by location, time, people, and tags.

5. Touch a photo to view it.

6. Touch to switch between the Grid and Filmstrip views.

7. Touch to return to the main Gallery app screen.

Reviewing and Sharing Pictures and Videos

After you open a photo, you can review it and share it with your friends.

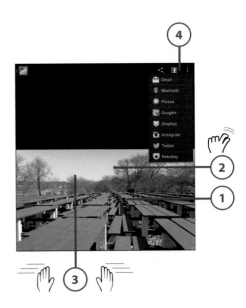

1. Double-tap the picture to zoom in to the maximum zoom level. Double-tap again to zoom all the way back to 100%.

2. Use the pinch gesture to have a more controlled zoom in and zoom out.

3. Scroll left and right to see all the photos in the album.

4. Touch to share the picture with friends using Facebook, Twitter, Gmail, Email, Google+, Picasa (Google Photos), and more.

Use Photo as Wallpaper or Contact Picture

While viewing a photo, touch the Menu button and choose Set Picture As. You can choose to use the photo as a contact picture for one of your contacts, or use it as the wallpaper on the Home screen.

Touch to use the picture   **Touch Menu**

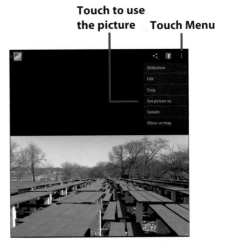

Can I Share a Photo Sphere?

You can share a Photo Sphere in one of two ways: as an interactive Photo Sphere, where the viewer can move around your Sphere interactively, or as a static image. Google+ is currently the only place that supports interactive Photo Sphere uploads. All other photo-sharing services and social networks such as Facebook and Twitter only support static images.

Editing Pictures

You can edit a picture by adding filters to it, enhancing it, or cropping it. These steps apply to still pictures, panoramic pictures, and Photo Sphere pictures.

1. Touch the Menu button.

2. Touch Edit.

3. Touch to apply one or more filters to the picture.

4. Touch to apply frames and borders to the picture.

5. Touch to crop the picture, straighten it, rotate it, or apply a mirror image effect to it.

6. Touch to apply additional effects to the picture including enhancing shadows, changing the sharpness of the picture, color saturation, and more.

Go directly to cropping

Touch as a quicker way to get to the Edit screen

7. Touch the Menu button to undo or redo your edits.

8. Touch to undo changes you have made to a photo one-by-one. If you have made multiple changes, you can repeatedly touch the Undo icon until you have removed all changes.

9. Touch to redo a change that you have undone.

10. Touch reset the picture to its original state.

11. Touch to save your edited photo. Edited photos are placed in a new album called Edited Online Photos so that the original photo remains intact.

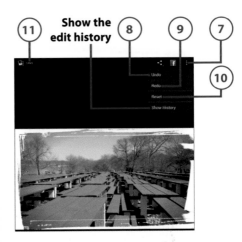

Show the edit history

The Tiny Planet Effect

While viewing a Photo Sphere picture, you can apply the Tiny Planet effect to it. The Tiny Planet effect takes your Photo Sphere and wraps it around an tiny imaginary planet. The result is a very cool picture that has the buildings in your Photo Sphere towering over the tiny planet. To apply the Tiny Planet effect, while viewing the Photo Sphere, touch the screen anywhere to reveal the Tiny Planet icon. Touch it and use the slider to increase or decrease the size of your tiny planet.

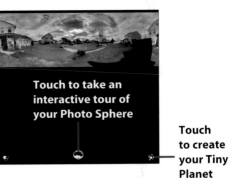

Touch to take an interactive tour of your Photo Sphere

Touch to create your Tiny Planet

Touch to use the picture

Touch Menu

Trimming Videos

You can trim a video that you have recorded on your Nexus 10 in the Gallery app. This is useful if you want to trim out unwanted portions and save only the relevant parts.

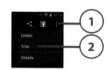

1. Touch the Menu button.

2. Touch Trim.

3. Slide the video play marker left and right to scrub quickly through the video and find the parts you want to trim out.

4. Slide the video start marker left and right to change the new starting point of the video.

5. Slide the video end marker left and right to change the new ending point of the video.

6. Touch to save the new trimmed video. The original video is unchanged and the new trimmed version is saved as a new video.

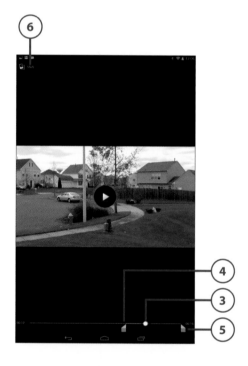

Modifying Gallery Settings

1. Touch the Menu button.

2. Touch Settings.

3. Touch to enable or disable synchronizing photos over Wi-Fi only. If you uncheck this box, photo synchronization occurs even when you are using a cellular data network if your Google Nexus Tablet supports cellular data.

4. Touch to edit a Google account or remove it.

5. Touch the Google account.

6. Touch to enable or disable synchronizing Google Photos for this Google account.

7. Touch the Menu button to reveal account actions.

8. Touch to remove the Google account.

9. Touch to manually synchronize the account.

10. Touch to save your changes and return to the previous screen.

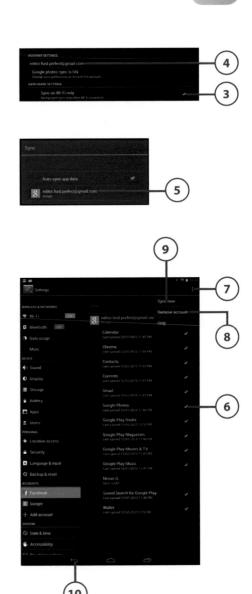

Managing Photos with Your Computer

When you connect your Google Nexus Tablet to a computer, you can move pictures back and forth manually by using software such as Android File Transfer. If you have not yet installed Android File Transfer, follow the installation steps in the "Prologue."

Manual Picture Management

This section covers moving pictures using the Android File Transfer app if you are using a Mac, or the media transfer functionality if you are using Windows.

1. Plug your Nexus Tablet into your computer using the supplied USB cable.

2. Pull down the Notification Bar to reveal the USB Connected notification.

3. Touch the Connected As a Media Device notification.

4. Touch to check the box next to Media Device (MTP), if it is not already checked.

Moving Pictures (Mac OSX)

After your Nexus Tablet is connected to your Mac, the Android File Transfer app automatically launches so you can browse the files on your phone as well as move or copy files between your Mac and your Nexus Tablet.

1. Browse to your Nexus Tablet to locate the pictures.

Where Are the Pictures?

Pictures taken with the Nexus Tablet's camera are in the folder DCIM\Camera. All other pictures are in a folder called Pictures. Photos that you have edited are in a folder called Edited.

---

2. Drag one or more pictures from your Nexus Tablet to a folder on your Mac.

3. Drag a folder filled with pictures on your Mac to the folder called Pictures on your Nexus Tablet to create a new Photo Album.

4. Drag one or more pictures from your Mac to the Pictures folder on your Nexus Tablet.

Moving Pictures (Windows)

After your Nexus Tablet is connected to your Windows computer and mounted, you can browse the Nexus Tablet just like any other drive on your computer.

1. Click if you want to import the pictures automatically.

2. Click to open an Explorer view and see the files on your Nexus Tablet.

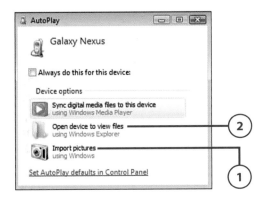

Where Are the Pictures?

Pictures taken with the Nexus Tablet's camera are in the folder DCIM\Camera. All other pictures are in a folder called Pictures. Photos that you have edited are in a folder called Edited.

3. Drag one or more pictures from your Nexus Tablet to a folder on your PC.

4. Drag a folder filled with pictures on your PC to the folder called Pictures on your Nexus Tablet to create a new Photo Album.

5. Drag one or more pictures from your PC to the Pictures folder on your Nexus Tablet.

Automatic Picture Management on a Mac

By setting your Nexus Tablet to connect as a Camera, your Mac automatically opens iPhoto.

1. Plug your Nexus Tablet into your computer using the supplied USB cable.

2. Pull down the System Bar to reveal the USB Connected notification.

3. Touch the Connected As a Media Device notification.

4. Touch to check the box next to Camera (PTP), if it is not already checked.

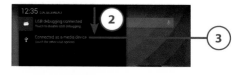

5. Your Nexus Tablet appears in iPhoto under Devices so that you can import photos like you would with any other digital camera.

Synchronizing Pictures Using Your Google Cloud

You can synchronize pictures to your Nexus Tablet from your computer without even connecting your phone to your computer. Just use your Google account's built-in cloud service. All photo albums that you create in the cloud are automatically synchronized to your Nexus Tablet.

1. Click Photos after you log in to Google on your desktop computer.

2. Click to see all the photos that have been automatically uploaded from your Galaxy Nexus to your Google Photos cloud account. When they display on the screen, you can download those pictures to your computer.

3. Click to manage your photo albums.

4. Click an existing photo album to open it, and add more photos to it from your computer.

5. Click to create a new photo album and add photos to it from your computer.

6. Type a name for your new photo album.

7. Click to browse your computer and choose photos to upload to the album.

8. Click to create the album.

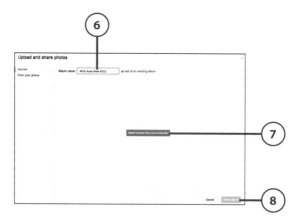

Index

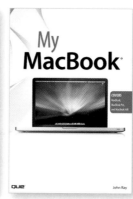

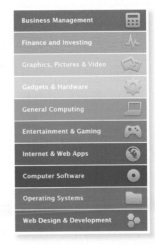

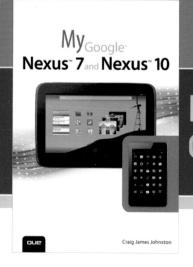

My Google
Nexus™ 7 and Nexus™ 10

que

Craig James Johnston

Safari.
Books Online

FREE
Online Edition

Your purchase of *My Google Nexus 7 and Nexus 10* includes access to a free online edition for 45 days through the **Safari Books Online** subscription service. Nearly every Que book is available online through **Safari Books Online**, along with thousands of books and videos from publishers such as Addison-Wesley Professional, Cisco Press, Exam Cram, IBM Press, O'Reilly Media, Prentice Hall, Sams, and VMware Press.

Safari Books Online is a digital library providing searchable, on-demand access to thousands of technology, digital media, and professional development books and videos from leading publishers. With one monthly or yearly subscription price, you get unlimited access to learning tools and information on topics including mobile app and software development, tips and tricks on using your favorite gadgets, networking, project management, graphic design, and much more.

Activate your FREE Online Edition at
informit.com/safarifree

STEP 1:   Enter the coupon code: VSFBXAA.

STEP 2:   New Safari users, complete the brief registration form.
Safari subscribers, just log in.

If you have difficulty registering on Safari or accessing the online edition,
please e-mail customer-service@safaribooksonline.com